BESTIARY

ESTI ARY

BEING AN
ENGLISH VERSION
OF THE BODLEIAN
LIBRARY, OXFORD
M. S. BODLEY 764

WITH ALL THE ORIGINAL MINIATURES
REPRODUCED IN FACSIMILE. TRANSLATED
AND INTRODUCED BY RICHARD BARBER.
THE BOYDELL PRESS. WOODBRIDGE. 1999

First published 1992
The Folio Society

Reissued 1993
The Boydell Press, Woodbridge
Reprinted in paperback 1999, 2006

ISBN 0 85115 329 1 hardback
ISBN 0 85115 753 X paperback

The Boydell Press is an imprint of Boydell & Brewer Ltd
PO Box 9, Woodbridge, Suffolk IP12 3DF, UK
and of Boydell & Brewer Inc.
668 Mt Hope Avenue, Rochester, NY 14620, USA
website: www.boydellandbrewer.com

A catalogue record for this book is available
from the British Library

Library of Congress Catalog Card Number: 92–2466

All the illustrations in this book
have been reproduced from MS. Bodley 364
by kind permission of
the Bodleian Library, University of Oxford

Printed in China by
Compass Press

CONTENTS

offers us a unique insight into the medieval mind. If we are to begin to understand it, we must lay aside all the mental attitudes we have accumulated from writers and thinkers since the Renaissance, and abandon the ideas on which modern science is founded. For the bestiary is an account of the natural world, which, although it goes back to those same Greek philosophers from whom our scientific concepts ultimately derive, looks at nature in a very different light. We find in it a description of a number of beasts, birds or fishes, varying from the instantly recognisable to the wholly fantastic, but the details are very rarely based on observation, on the experiences of the everyday world. Instead, the text is taken from *auctores*, writers recognised as authorities on the subject. It is as if each description began 'I have it on good authority...' Whether it is a question of a salamander that lives in fire or a cat that catches mice, the appeal is not to the evidence of our eyes, but to the books in the scribe's library.

For the object of the bestiary is not to document the natural world and to analyse it in order to understand its workings. The writers of bestiaries knew the laws of nature before they began their work, and were concerned only to expound them. They knew that everything in Creation had a purpose, and that the Creator had made nothing without an ulterior aim in mind. And they knew, too, what that purpose was: the edification and instruction of sinful man. The Creator had made animals, birds and fishes, and had given them their natures or habits, so that the sinner could see the world of mankind reflected in the kingdom of nature, and learn the way to redemption by the examples of different creatures. Each creature is therefore a kind of moral entity, bearing a message for the human reader.

Beyond the natural lore and moral meaning is a third aspect: the mystical significance of each creature, as reflected in Holy Scripture. While the relationship between nature and morality is often relatively straightforward, and the example is plain enough for even our obtuse twentieth-century minds to grasp, the mystical significance was much more of a problem for the compiler of the bestiary, because the same creature might well represent both good and evil, Christ or the devil, in different texts from the Bible. Confusion often ensued, and the writer was reduced to attributing two meanings to the same beast, one good and one evil, with several shades of probable meaning between the two extremes as well.

If the bestiary was a book which depended on authorities, what were these authorities to whom the writers of bestiaries appealed? Their immediate source was usually an earlier bestiary. In the case of the present text, which is found in two manuscripts written between 1220 and 1250, the compiler has taken as his main exemplar a manuscript written in the late twelfth century and has added excerpts from a treatise on beasts which forms part of Rabanus Maurus's *On the Nature of Things*, which includes a large number of references to Scripture. He has also included some good stories from Gerald of Wales's *Topography of Ireland*, about badgers, barnacle geese and other Irish birds, and has plundered Hugh of Fouilloy's *The Aviary* and Peter of Cornwall's *Pantheologus* as well. The last three works were quite recent, but the bestiary itself and Rabanus Maurus were much older: Rabanus was a German monk who wrote at the end of the eighth century, and he in turn owed much to Isidore of Seville's great encyclopedia called *Etymologies*, written in the sixth century. This explains why so many entries begin with an attempt to explain the name of the beast, often garbled and with a smattering of Greek, a language largely unknown in thirteenth-century England. Where Latin and Greek are quoted in the text to illustrate etymologies, the original is given exactly as in the manuscript, and is often, after centuries of copying, mere nonsense.

Behind the work of Isidore, one of the key texts of medieval learning, and behind the bestiary itself, there lay a common ancestor, the book called *Physiologus*, a Latin text which had been translated from the Greek into Latin at much the same time that Isidore was writing. The *Physiologus* is still present in our thirteenth-century version as the ultimate authority: 'Physiologus tells us ...' 'Physiologus says ...' writes our compiler. I have translated Physiologus as 'the naturalists', because the

Physiologus represents a Christian version of the accumulated knowledge of the natural historians of the ancient world. The Greek text of the *Physiologus* was put together in Alexandria, the home of knowledge *par excellence* where pagan and Christian learning met and mingled, at some time between the second and fifth centuries AD. The inheritance of the Classical world was, so to speak, frozen, or rather, preserved in a kind of Christian aspic, until the Renaissance; the recorded habits of the beasts were fixed as unwavering traditions, and only the commentary varied.

The *Physiologus* was enormously popular; if we include the bestiary as being a version of it, 'perhaps no book, except the Bible, has ever been so widely diffused among so many people and for so many centuries as the *Physiologus*. It has been translated into Latin, Ethiopic, Arabic, Armenian, Syriac, Anglo-Saxon, Icelandic, Spanish, Italian, Provencal and all the principal dialects of the Germanic and Romanic languages'.

The *Physiologus* was an attempt to redefine the natural world in Christian terms; and its material was drawn from the Greek philosophers and their Latin followers, notably Aristotle, Pliny and lesser luminaries such as C. Julius Solinus and Lucan. These were very different texts, scientific or poetic descriptions of the natural world, based on observation, a hesitant attempt to collect data from which an analysis of man's environment might begin. But the grain of literal truth in the bestiary is very much the grain of sand around which the pearl forms. To take a simple example: the unicorn probably arises from a Greek traveller's misreading of Persian sculpture such as that at Persepolis, where bulls and other horned animals are represented in low relief but from a strictly two-dimensional perspective, so that two horns become one. Other fantastic beasts are echoes of symbolism from Oriental art: the winged lions develop into gryphons, the man-headed beasts of Persian art grow into the manticore, and the parijata tree becomes the perindens. For other creatures, a real but misinterpreted habit may be at the root of the imaginative development of a being that never was: modern naturalists have observed the phenomenon of 'anting' in birds, during which they will approach fire and emerge unscathed, phoenix-like. Other stories, such as the gold-digging ants of Ethiopia, are the products of too much learning and too little lore: their name is *myrmeco-leon*, which was Latinised as 'ant-lion', *myrmex* being the Greek for ant. The animal which the original writer had in mind was probably the honey-badger, and the Ethiopian gold was simply the honey which it digs out of the ground and on which it feasts. Other stories were elaborated as they passed from author to author: the tigress deceived by her image in a glass sphere goes back to an anecdote in Pliny's *Natural History* as retold by St Ambrose in his *Hexaemeron*. The yale, with its movable horns, has been traced back to African tribes who train one horn of their cattle forward and the other backward; the curious appearance of these beasts would have led travellers to believe that the cattle themselves could point their horns at will in any direction they pleased. But such reconstructions are a matter of guesswork; another recent book firmly insists that the yale is the Indian water-buffalo, introduced into England by Richard of Cornwall, brother of Henry III, in the mid-thirteenth century.

The bestiary is not simply a book of marvels, a collection of fantasies. Less than a tenth of its space is given up to creatures of a kind that the artists used to fill the blanks of their maps with 'Here be monsters'. Monsters *are* here, but very much in a minority. For what is the good of a lesson that can only be taught by hearsay, relating to a beast that no one has ever seen in the flesh? The longest sermons are devoted to topics drawn from everyday life: the ant and the bee display the virtues of humility, obedience and industry, the viper warns against the sin of adultery. Of particular interest is the attention given to falcons and horses, because these were the enthusiasms of the nobility, and many of the illustrated manuscripts written in England may have been produced for members of the nobility, whether abbots or lay patrons. In the case of the present manuscript, it may well have had a lay patron, for in the miniature of the elephant the shields hung on the castle on its back show recognisable coats of arms. In the centre is *azure, a lion rampant argent*; to the right, *or, three chevrons gules*; to the left, *or, a bend cotised gules*; and on a pennant at the front of the tower, the arms are *gules, a chevron argent*. Three of the four shields can be positively identified as belonging to barons with lands on the Welsh marches. The centre shield belonged to Roger de Monhaut; the Berkeley arms are on the right-hand shield, and the arms of Clare are on the pennant. The left-hand shield is a problem, but could be that of the Bohun family, earls of Hereford. Given the relative prominence of the different arms, it looks as if Roger de Monhaut, whose shield is in the centre, commissioned the book, but it could also be the Berkeley family. The miniature makes this one of the earliest examples of a manuscript which contains a heraldic reference to the family for whom it was made, a device which was common in the fourteenth century.

The bestiary was an obvious subject for illustration, and a copy of the Greek version from the eleventh century has illustrations which may represent a tradition going back to the period before the controversy over images in the Orthodox church, when in the seventh century the iconoclasts attacked all representations of sacred subjects in art. Some, but not all, of these pictures were taken over in the Latin versions of the *Physiologus*, and a good proportion of all the Latin texts have some kind of illustration. Creatures from the bestiary appear in their traditional roles in the borders of the Bayeux tapestry, and are widespread in Romanesque and Gothic art. There is a fascinating contrast between text and miniatures in our manuscript: the text tells very little about the cat, for example, but the artist tells us that it will try to get at a bird in a cage, loves to sleep by the fire, and shows it on a background of moon and stars to indicate its nocturnal habits. In two other cases the artist has solved a problem presented by the text by illustrating two different creatures when the text gives the same name but different descriptions: these are the screech-owl (ulula) and the hoopoe (epopus/upupa).

Richly illuminated bestiaries are a peculiarly English phenomenon, and reached their apogee in the first half of the thirteenth century. The Ashmole bestiary, now in the Bodleian Library, with its lavish use of gold grounds, is perhaps the most luxurious and expensively produced copy. But the manuscript (Bodley 764) whose miniatures are reproduced here is artistically much more lively; it is two or three decades later than the Ashmole volume, and the Gothic style has moved on, into a more free and naturalistic world, with dazzling use of colour replacing the glow of the gold. Just as the text derives from earlier copies with variations, so the composition of the pictures can be traced back to earlier copies: there is a closely-related manuscript in the British Library (Harley 4751), which may have been produced at Salisbury. This in turn derives from a bestiary illustrated with outline drawings, which may or may not have been intended for painting; the manuscript is now at Cambridge, and was the text which T.H. White used for his notable version of the bestiary, *The Book of Beasts*. The style of the Cambridge volume harks back to that of twelfth-century book illumination, where colour was often not used, or was restricted to a wash background.

In all of those manuscripts, the subjects are often closely copied from each other: the most striking instance is the whale, for which not only the Cambridge, Harley and Bodley manuscripts, but also a bestiary until recently at Alnwick Castle, have an almost identical picture. These illuminated de luxe bestiaries are clearly a close-knit group, produced in a relatively short period, perhaps through the enthusiasm of a small number of artists and their patrons. From the fourteenth century onwards, books of hours became the focus for luxury productions for individual owners, but these were much more personal, because they were books for private devotion, and often in daily use. There is no clear explanation as to why this fascinating group of copies of the bestiary should have come into existence, or why it did not continue to flourish. Perhaps we can claim the fantastic 'babewynes' which lurk in the borders of fourteenth-century English manuscripts such as the Luttrell Psalter as the descendants of the luxury bestiaries.

The contents of the bestiary, as we have already indicated, varied with each successive manuscript; it is the exception rather than the rule to find two manuscripts with texts that are nearly identical. The *Physiologus* was a short and relatively stable text, and the main Continental versions do not vary greatly. The earliest English bestiaries, such as one which may have come

from Christchurch, Canterbury (Bodleian Library, MS Laud Misc.
247) were no more and no less than versions of the *Physiologus* in
Latin, but with the crucial difference that additions from Isidore of
Seville's *Etymologies* were included. At this point, the original text
ceased to be sacred; and once the idea that it could be augmented
took hold, the bestiary rapidly attracted all kinds of new material.
The original Latin version of the *Physiologus* had thirty-nine
chapters, while the most expansive thirteenth-century bestiaries
had grown to four times that length. Much of this expansion, as
the late Brunsdon Yapp pointed out, is due to the addition of
northern fauna to the essentially north African creatures in the
original *Physiologus*. The new entries in the English bestiaries are
generally familiar creatures, though a few fresh curiosities such
as the yale and the rhinoceros creep in. The present manuscript
and its twin, Harley 4751, have entries for the sow, badger,
tragelaphus, and hare which are not in earlier texts, and which
rarely reappear at a later date. A similar pattern applies to the
birds; the largest number of additions are in the first English
bestiaries, while our text augments these with the Irish birds from
Gerald of Wales's *Topography of Ireland*. However, the basic struc-
ture remained – description, moral, meaning – even though the
neat colophon of each *Physiologus* entry ('Well, therefore, did the
Physiologus speak concerning the lion', or whale, or amphisbaena) disappeared among the enthusiastic collection of biblical
references.

The most important step forward was when someone, probably
in the late twelfth century, decided to group the entries by type,
and to classify them as beasts, birds, snakes and fishes, and to
expand greatly the contents, going back to either Isidore of Seville
or Rabanus Maurus, who had himself derived most of his material
from Isidore, but had added his own moralisings and biblical
quotations. The present manuscript has particularly large
extracts from Rabanus. Some apparently random insertions
became traditional: in the section about dogs, a stray sermon
beginning 'Whatsoever sinner ...' has attached itself to the
text, but breaks off incomplete. It is found, with no apparent
recognition that it is an anomaly, in a number of manuscripts

which are by no means identical copies. It does imply that the scribe was not usually responsible for the selection of material to be included in the bestiary, or he would have edited out this part: instead, it seems as if the compiler told the scribe to copy out the basic bestiary text (by now including the sermon) and to add the passages he indicated from other books. In our text, the entries are in better order, because it starts with the general observations about animals, which are often found after most of the animals have been described.

The Latin of the bestiary is distinctly problematic. It contains words found nowhere else, and because the writers – whoever they may have been among the many hands that contributed over the centuries – are often trying to describe things about which they are unsure, the text is often obscure, and all translators who have attempted a rendering into modern languages have ended up by admitting to a degree of intelligent guesswork rather than an absolutely certain equivalent. In identifying the beasts, which is often very difficult, I have in general followed the modern equivalents set out by Wilma George and Brunsdon Yapp in their very useful study of the bestiary, *The Naming of the Beasts*.

If the content and meaning are a problem, so is the style. I have settled for a version which is straightforward, with perhaps an echo of the language of the Authorised Version, rather than a colloquial rendering, because this seems closer to the spirit of the work. It is after all a work which takes a high moral tone, and preaches at its reader; so I have treated it as a sermon rather than as a series of anecdotes. T.H. White wrote of the text which he translated that the original 'sometimes gives the impression of having been written by a schoolboy who has suffered a course of Bible reading'. This is more than a little unfair: the author would have been more than a match for Macaulay's omniscient schoolboy, and in the case of our text the quotations from Rabanus Maurus can only be described as being an attempt at a kind of high style. I hope I have caught something of the voice of the original; I am sure that it is at any rate a serious voice. (Much as I admire T.H. White's work, I think he does the original an injustice when he lightens the tone: his parrot says 'What-cheer?' or

'Toodle-oo!' for the Latin and Greek equivalents of 'Hallo'.) But I have taken the same liberties as he did with the text in the interest of ease of reading, and have not annotated the many silent amendments which have to be made to arrive at a readable version. (There is no critical edition of the later versions of the bestiary to which the translator can turn, and the first task was indeed to establish a working Latin text.)

From the outset, it was intended that this edition should use the layout of the original manuscript; the miniatures are reproduced to their original size and in their original positions on the page, so that what appears in the following pages was designed by a thirteenth-century scribe and his illuminator, the only change being that the text is in a modern typeface rather than a highly abbreviated formal Gothic book-hand. As a result, and because the English equivalent comes out longer than the Latin text, discreet cutting of the text has been necessary, and I hope that the reader will pardon this. Fortunately, because the author quotes Scriptural examples so freely towards the end of each entry, the effect is perhaps to redress the balance of natural history, morality and mystical meaning in favour of natural history; very little of the text describing the inhabitants of the bestiary has been omitted.

The work which follows can be read and enjoyed on many levels. It will entertain as a collection of curious lore; it will edify as a series of moral examples; it will lead us, if we wish, into a world reminiscent of Jungian symbolism, with a Christian gloss; and it will delight the eye with some of the most charming miniatures to be found in any medieval manuscript.

SUGGESTIONS FOR FURTHER READING: BOOKS ON THE BESTIARY
are few and far between; the most accessible are T.H. White's
translation *The Book of Beasts* (London 1954) and Wilma George
and Brunsdon Yapp's *The Naming of the Beasts* (London 1991).
M.R. James's introduction to the facsimile of the Cambridge
bestiary manuscript (Cambridge University Library Ii.4.26) is
unfortunately only available in the very rare Roxburghe Club
edition (London 1928), and the only other general work is by an
American scholar, Florence McCulloch (*Medieval Bestiaries*,
Philadelphia 1962; not published in Britain).

BESTIARY

living beings a designation, calling each by a name which corresponded to the present order and according to their nature and function. The heathens, however, gave each beast a name in their own language. But Adam gave them names, not in Greek or Latin, nor in any of the languages of the barbarian peoples, but in that language which was common to all peoples before the Flood, and which is called Hebrew. In Latin they are called animals or animate beings, because they are animated by life and moved by breath. Quadrupeds are so called because they go on four feet (quatuor pedibus); although they are like cattle, they are not under man's control. Quadrupeds are deer, fallow deer, wild asses and so on. But they are not wild beasts like lions, nor domestic animals which help men in their labours. Everything that lacks a human face and tongue we call cattle. In its strict sense, however, cattle is usually reserved for those beasts which are suitable for food, such as sheep and pigs, or which are used by men, such as horses and oxen. But there is a distinction between cattle in general (pecora) and edible cattle (pecudes). Men of old used the description cattle of all animals. 'Pecudes' are only those animals which you eat (pecu edes). All grazing animals are called 'pecus' because they graze (a pascendo). Beasts of burden are so called because they bear our burdens by helping us to carry loads or to plough: oxen pull the loaded wagon and turn the hardest soil with the plough. Horses and asses carry men and ease their progress when they travel. So they are called beasts of burden, because they carry men's burdens. They are very strong beasts. Oxen are called yoke-cattle (armenta) because they are suited for arms, i.e. warfare, or because they are used in armed warfare. Others say it is because they plough (ab arando) or because they are 'armed' with horns. There is a distinction between yoke-cattle and herds. Horses and oxen belong to yoke-cattle, while herds are made up of goats and sheep.

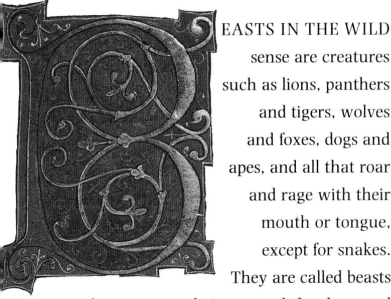

sense are creatures such as lions, panthers and tigers, wolves and foxes, dogs and apes, and all that roar and rage with their mouth or tongue, except for snakes. They are called beasts because they possess their natural freedom and act as they themselves have willed. Their will is indeed free and they range hither and thither; where their instinct leads them, there they go. The name lion is of Greek origin, and was taken into Latin. In Greek the lion is called 'leon', and it is partly corrupted in Latin. For 'leo' in Greek means 'king' in Latin, and he is so called because he is the king of beasts. There are three kinds of lion; of these, the short ones with curly manes are peaceful, the long ones with smooth hair are fierce; their brow and tail show their temperament. Their courage is in their breast, their strength in their head. They fear the noise of wheels, but fire frightens them even more. The lion is proud by nature; he will not live with other kinds of beasts in the wild, but like a king

24 disdains the company of the masses. ¶Naturalists tell us that the lion has three chief characteristics. The first is that he loves to roam the mountain-tops. If it so happens that hunters come in search of him, the scent of the hunters reaches him and he wipes out his tracks behind him with his tail, lest the hunters follow him, find his lair, and take him. So our Redeemer, the spiritual lion of the tribe of Judah, the root of Jesse, the son of David, hid the tracks of His love in heaven, until, sent by the Father, He descended into the womb of the Virgin Mary, and redeemed lost mankind. And the devil, the enemy of mankind, did not know this and dared to tempt Him like an ordinary man. Even the angels in the height did not know it, and said to those who were with Him, as He ascended to the Father: 'Who is this King of Glory?' ¶His second characteristic is that he seems to have his eyes open when he sleeps. So our Lord, who fell asleep within the body on the Cross, and was buried while His Godhead kept watch, as it says in the Song of Songs: 'I sleep, but my heart waketh' [5:2]. And in the psalm: 'He who keepeth Israel shall neither slumber nor sleep' [121:4]. ¶His third characteristic is that when the lioness brings forth her cubs, they come into the world dead. She watches over them for three days, until on the third

day the father comes, blows in their faces, and awakens them to life. In the same way the Almighty Father awoke our Lord Jesus Christ from the dead on the third day, as Jacob says: 'He couched as a lion; who shall rouse him up?' [Genesis 49:9]. The nature of the lion is such that he is not enraged by men if he is not harmed by them. Unreasonable men should learn by this example; for men grow angry even when they are not harmed, and oppress the innocent, against the Christian commandment that even the guilty should go free. The merciful nature of lions is confirmed by numerous examples: they will spare men lying on the ground, and will lead captives whom they meet to their home. They will attack men rather than women. They only kill children if they are exceptionally hungry. Equally, they will abstain from eating to excess, particularly as they drink on one day, and take food on the next. And if they do not digest it, they refrain from eating for a day. And if they have difficulty with too much meat, they will put a paw in their mouth, and pull it out of their own free will. They do the same if they are full and have to take flight. You can tell an old lion by his lack of teeth. They mate face to face, as also do the lynx, camel, elephant, and rhinoceros. When a lioness gives birth for the first time, she gives birth to five cubs. Each year the number grows less, and when she has given birth to only one, she is no longer fertile, and remains sterile from then on. The lion rejects yesterday's food and turns away from food which he himself has left from a previous meal. Which animal dares to resist him whose voice is by its nature terror itself, so that many animals who could escape him by virtue of their speed are so terrified by his roaring that they are already vanquished? A sick lion will seek out an ape and devour it in order to be cured. The lion fears cocks, especially white cocks. Although the lion is the king of beasts, he is terrified of the tiny sting of a scorpion, and can be killed by a snake's poison. We call certain very small creatures 'lion-killers': they are caught and burnt, and that meat which is smeared with their ashes and left at a crossroads will kill lions even if they only eat a little of it. For this reason lions pursue 'lion-killers' as their natural

enemies, and if they possibly can, they avoid biting them, but trample them underfoot.

¶The lioness stands for the human mind when Job says: 'You have caught me because of my pride, like a lioness.' The divine dispensation uses everything around us for its own purposes, and allows our flesh to be harried by adversity lest in security our minds become presumptuous and puffed up with pride, and so that while we are in trouble, we place greater faith in the help of our Creator alone. Hence it is well said: 'You have caught me because of my pride, like a lioness.' For the lioness, when she seeks food for her cubs, lurks in ditches to capture her prey. In various places it is reported that men dig a pit on her accustomed path and place a sheep in it, in order to tempt the lioness's appetite. The pit is narrow and steep-sided, so that once the lioness is in it there is no way in which she can jump out. A second deep pit is dug adjoining the first, and the sheep is placed at the opposite end. There is also a cave in it, because when the lioness falls in the other pit, the sheep is terrified and willingly hides in the cave. And it comes to no harm, but is retrieved safely by shutting off the cave.

¶Thus the human mind, while seeking to feed carnal appetites, is caught in the trap which is concealed by freedom of choice, just as the lioness seeks food

for her cubs and is killed in the pit intended to deceive her, because her enemies persuade her to reach out her paw for forbidden food.

¶The tiger is named after its swift flight; the Persians, Greeks and Medes call it 'the arrow'. It is a beast with colourful spots, of extraordinary qualities and swiftness, after which the River Tigris is named because it is the swiftest of all rivers. The chief home of the tiger is around the Caspian Sea. If a tigress finds her lair robbed of its cubs, she sets out at once in pursuit of the thief. When the latter, even if he is mounted on a swift horse, realises that he is being overtaken by the speed of the beast, and has no other means of escape, he will use this ingenious deception. As soon as he sees that the tigress is near him, he throws down a glass sphere. The tigress is deceived by the image in it, and believes it is her cub. She halts in her tracks and tries to pick up the cub. Delayed by the false appearance, she redoubles her speed in pursuit of the rider, spurred on by her fury. But he throws down another sphere, which delays her again, because the memory of the deception is overcome by her maternal instinct. She turns the hollow image and sits down as if to suckle her cub. So the intensity of her motherly love betrays her, and deprives her of both her revenge and her cub.

¶There is an animal called the panther, which is brightly coloured, very beautiful and tame. Natural historians say that his only enemy is the dragon. When he has eaten and is full, he hides in his lair and sleeps. After three days he rouses himself from sleep, and lets forth a great roar; and out of his mouth comes a very sweet smell that seems to contain every kind of scent. When the other animals hear his voice they gather from far and near, and follow him wherever he goes on account of the sweetness of his breath. Only the dragon, hearing his voice, hides in terror in the bowels of the earth. There it lies in a daze, because it cannot bear the sweet smell, and remains motionless, as if it were dead. The other animals follow the panther wherever he goes. ¶Thus our Lord Jesus Christ, the true panther, descended from heaven and saved us from the power of the devil. 'When He ascended up on high, He led captivity captive and gave gifts unto men' [Ephesians 4:8]. The panther's bright colours remind us what Solomon said of Christ, who is the wisdom of God the Father: 'An understanding spirit, holy, one only, manifold, subtle, lively, clear, undefiled, plain, not subject to hurt, loving the thing that is good' [Wisdom 7:22]. It is a beautiful beast, just as David said of Christ: 'Thou art fairer than the children of men' [Psalm 45:2]. It is a tame beast, as Isaiah [Zechariah] said: 'Rejoice greatly, O daughter of Zion; shout, O daughter of Jerusalem: behold, thy King cometh unto thee' [9:9]. As soon as He is sated, He conceals his true self in the mockery of the Jews, the floggings, blows, injustice, scorn and thorns; He is hung from the cross by His hands, pierced with nails, given gall and vinegar to drink and wounded with the lance. He falls asleep and rests in the grave, and descends to the underworld, where He chains the great dragon. On the third day He rises from sleep and sends out a great cry and pours out sweetness, as David says: 'Then the Lord awakened as one out of sleep, and like a mighty man that shouteth by reason of wine' [Psalm 78:65]. And He cries with a loud voice, so that the sound is heard in all the world, His words carry to the ends of the earth. And just as sweet breath issues from the panther's mouth and all the animals gather from far and near and follow him, so the Jews, who sometimes thought like animals but were near to Him through their law, also heard Him, and the heathens too, far off and beyond the Law; they all heard Christ's voice and followed Him, saying with the prophet: 'How sweet are Thy words unto my taste! yea, sweeter than honey to my mouth' [Psalm 119:103]. It was also said of Him: 'Grace is poured into Thy lips; therefore God hath blessed Thee for ever' [Psalm 45:2]. And Solomon said: 'How much better is ... the smell of Thine ointments than all spices!' [Song of Songs 4:10]. And again: 'We follow the sweet scent of Thine ointments'; and a little later: 'The King hath brought me into His chamber' [Song of Songs 1:4]. We must pursue the sweet scent of Christ's commandments as quickly as we can, like the young girls who are the souls received in baptism; and we must turn from earthly to heavenly things, so that the King leads us into His place, into Jerusalem, the city of the Lord of hosts, the mountain of all the saints. ¶The panther is a beast marked with little circles of colour, like eyes with yellow, white and black circles. The female only gives birth once, for a good reason. Once the three cubs have grown within their mother's body until they are strong enough to be born, they hate having to stay there any longer. They scratch with their claws at the womb which is laden with its fruit, as if it prevented them from being born. The mother, overcome with pain, pushes them out and after this the seed which penetrates into the scarred and distorted womb does not take root, but flows out again unused. Pliny says that animals with sharp claws cannot bear cubs often because they are badly wounded internally by the movement of their young.

¶There is an animal called the antelope, with very keen hearing, so that no hunter can approach it. It has long horns like a saw so that it can saw down great tall trees and fell them to the ground. If it is thirsty it goes to the River Euphrates. There is a bush there called 'hedgehog-bush' in Greek which has a mass of thin and entwined twigs. The animal begins to play with it with its horns, and in playing it entangles itself by the horns in the twigs. When it has struggled for a long while, it cannot free itself, and cries out loudly. As soon as the hunter hears its cry, he comes and kills it. ¶So it is with you, O man, who tries to be sober and chaste and to lead a holy life: the two Testaments serve you as two horns, with the help of which you can fell and root out all bodily and spiritual vices. Beware of drunkenness, lest you are entangled in the snares of lust and slain by the devil; for 'wine and women will make men of understanding to fall away' [Ecclesiasticus 19:2].

¶The pard is a mottled beast and very swift, thirsty for blood; if it pounces, it kills. The leopard is born of an adulterous match between a lioness and a pard, from which a third kind of beast is born, as Pliny says in his Natural History: a lion can mate with a female pard, and a male pard with a lioness, and from both matings comes a degenerate creature like a mule or an ass. The mystic pard signifies either the devil, full of a diversity of vices, or the sinner, spotted with crimes and a variety of wrongdoings. Hence the prophet says: 'Can the Ethiopian change his skin, or the leopard his spots?' [Jeremiah 13:23]. Antichrist is known as a pard, spotted with many kinds of evil, in the Apocalypse: 'And the beast which I saw was like unto a leopard' [Revelations 13:2]; the same has been said of those who persisted in the blackness of sins and a variety of wrong-doings. Elsewhere it is written: 'The wolf also shall dwell with the lamb, and the leopard shall lie down with the kid' [Isaiah 11:6]. And this was accomplished in Christ's coming, when they who had previously been fierce lived with the innocent, and those who were spotted with wrongdoings were converted through repentance to the true faith.

¶The unicorn, which is also called rhinoceros in Greek, has this nature: it is a little beast, not unlike a young goat, and extraordinarily swift. It has a horn in the middle of its brow, and no hunter can catch it. But it can be caught in the following fashion: a girl who is a virgin is led to the place where it dwells, and is left there alone in the forest. As soon as the unicorn sees her, it leaps into her lap and embraces her, and goes to sleep there; then the hunters capture it and display it in the king's palace. Our Lord Jesus Christ is the spiritual unicorn of whom it is said: 'My beloved is like the son of the unicorns' [Song of Songs 2:9]; and in the psalm: 'My horn shalt thou exalt like the horn of an unicorn' [92:10]; and Zacharias said: 'He hath raised up an horn of salvation for us, in the house of His servant David' [Luke 1:69]. The single horn on the unicorn's head signifies what He Himself said: 'I and my Father are one' [John 10:30]; according to the Apostle, 'The head of Christ is God' [I Corinthians 11:3]. He is called very swift, for neither principalities nor powers, nor thrones nor lordships could capture Him; the underworld could not hold Him, and not even the most cunning devil could understand Him. But by the will of the Father alone He descended into the Virgin's womb to save us. He is called an insignificant creature because He humbled Himself in the flesh: He Himself said: 'Learn of me, for I am meek and lowly in heart' [Matthew 11:29]. The unicorn often fights elephants; it wounds them in the stomach and kills them.

38 ¶The lynx is so called because it is counted as a kind of wolf (lupus). It is a beast marked with spots on its back like those of a pard, but it resembles a wolf: its urine is said to harden into a valuable jewel called ligurius. The lynxes know that this is valuable, as is proved by the exceptional care with which they cover it with sand: they are naturally jealous, and cannot bear it to fall into the hands of man. Pliny says that lynxes only bear cubs once. This beast typifies envious men who, in the hard-ness of their hearts, would rather do harm than good and are intent on worldly desires: even things for which they have no use and which might benefit others they render useless.

¶The gryphon is at once feathered and four-footed.
It lives in the south and in mountains. The hinder
part of its body is like a lion; its wings and face are
like an eagle. It hates the horse bitterly and if it
comes face to face with a man, it will attack him.

¶There is an animal called the elephant, which has
no desire to mate. The Greeks believe that the name

of the elephant comes from the size of his body, because he looks like a mountain: 'elephio' is the Greek for mountain. The Indians call him 'barro' (bhri) from the sound of his voice: 'barritus' means the roar of an elephant, and 'ivory' the teeth of the elephant. His nose is called a trunk because he uses it to put food in his mouth; the trunk is like a snake and is protected by a rampart of ivory. There is no beast greater than this. The Persians and Indians put wooden towers on his back and fight with arrows as if they were on top of a wall. Elephants have a lively intelligence and memory. They move about in herds, flee from mice, and mate with their backs to each other. Pregnancy lasts for two years; nor do they give birth more than once, and never to several young, but to only one. They live for three hundred years. If, however, they want to have off-spring, they go to the east, near the earthly paradise, where a tree called mandragora grows. The elephant and his mate go there, and she picks a fruit from the tree and gives it to him. And she seduces him into eating it; after they have both eaten it, they mate and the female at once conceives. When the time comes for her to give birth, she goes to a pond, and the water comes up to her udder. The male elephant guards her while she gives birth, because

the dragon is the enemy of the elephant. If the
elephant finds a snake he will kill it by trampling on
it until it is dead. The elephant strikes terror into
bulls, and yet is terrified by a mouse. His nature is
such that, if he falls down, he cannot stand up again.
Yet he will fall if he leans against a tree in order to
sleep. For he has no joints in his knees, and the
hunter cuts a little way into the tree, so that as soon
as the elephant leans against it, he falls with the tree.
When he falls, he trumpets loudly, and at once a
huge elephant comes, but is unable to lift him. Then
they both trumpet together, and twelve elephants
come, and are unable to lift him. They all trumpet,
and at once a little elephant appears and puts his
trunk under the large elephant, and lifts him up. The
little elephant has the following characteristic:
wherever some of his hair and bones are burnt,
nothing evil can do harm, not even a dragon. ¶The
elephant and his wife represent Adam and his wife,
who pleased God in the flesh before their sin, and
knew nothing of mating or of sin. When the woman
ate of the tree, that is, gave the herb mandragora
which brought understanding to her husband, she
became pregnant and for that reason left paradise.
For as long as they were in paradise, Adam did not
know her in the flesh. For it is written: 'And Adam

knew Eve his wife; and she conceived' [Genesis 4:1] and bore a son amid the waters of shame of which the prophet says: 'Save me O God, for the waters are come in unto my soul' [Psalm 69:1]. And at once they were seduced by the dragon and banished from their haven, that is, they were no longer pleasing to God. Then the great elephant came, namely the Law, and could not help him to rise, any more than the priest could help the man who fell among thieves [Luke 10:30]. And even the twelve elephants (that is, all the prophets) could not help him, like the Levite and the wounded man of whom we spoke. But the cunning elephant, that is our Lord Jesus Christ, although He was greatest of all, became very small, in that He humbled Himself before death, in order to raise mankind up, a true compassionate Samaritan who set the man who had fallen among thieves on his beast of burden. For He Himself was wounded, and took upon Himself our weaknesses and bore our sins: the Samaritan means a guardian. But where God is present, the devil cannot come near. ¶Whatever an elephant picks up in its trunk it breaks, and what it tramples underfoot it crushes to death beneath the debris of a giant ruin. They never fight over their females, because adultery is unknown among them. The goodness of mercy is within them.

For when they see men wandering in the desert, they lead them back into familiar ways, and when they meet a flock of sheep huddling together they protect them on their journey, so that no missile kills any of them. If they fight in a battle, they always take great care of the weary and the wounded.

¶There is an animal called the beaver, which is quite tame, whose testicles are excellent as medicine. The naturalists say of it that when it realises that hunters are pursuing it, it bites off its testicles and throws them down in front of the hunters, and thus takes flight and escapes. If it so happens that another hunter follows it, it stands up on its hind legs and shows its sexual organs. When the second hunter sees that it has no testicles, he goes away. In like fashion everyone who reforms his life and wants to live chastely in accordance with God's commandments should cut off all vices and shameless deeds and throw them in the devil's face. Then the devil will see that that man has nothing belonging to him and will leave him, ashamed. That man will live in God, and will not be taken by the devil, who says: 'I will overtake, I will divide the spoil' [Exodus 15:9]. The beaver (castor) is so called because it castrates itself.

¶There is an animal called the ibex. This creature has two horns, which are so strong that if it falls from a high mountain down a precipice, its horns bear the whole weight of its body and it escapes unhurt. This beast represents those learned men who understand the harmony of the Old and New Testaments, and if anything untoward happens to them, they are supported as if on two horns by all the good they have derived from reading the witness of the Old Testament and the Gospels.

¶There is an animal called the hyena, which lives in the graves of dead men and feeds on their bodies. By nature it is sometimes masculine, sometimes feminine, and for that reason it is an unclean beast. It has a rigid spine, all in one piece, so it can only turn round by using its whole body. Solinus relates many marvellous things about this beast. First, it follows the shepherds when they move their sheepfolds, and creeps round men's houses at night. By dint of constant listening, it learns to call out and can imitate the human voice, so that it cunningly lures men outside and falls on them at night. It counterfeits human vomit and makes sounds like a man being sick to lure out dogs, so that it can devour them. If hounds happen to come into its shadow while hunting, they lose their voices and cannot give tongue. These hyenas dig up graves in their search for buried corpses. ¶The children of Israel are like this beast; at first they served the living God but later fell prey to riches and easy living and worshipped idols. Hence the prophets likened the Jewish people to an unclean beast, saying: 'Mine heritage is become as the hyena's lair' [Jeremiah 12:8]. Every one among us who serves riches and an easy life is like this animal, for they are neither men nor women, that is, neither believers nor unbelievers, but certainly belong to those of whom Solomon [St James] says 'a double-minded man, unstable in all his ways' [James 1:8]. The Lord said of them: 'Ye cannot serve God and Mammon' [Matthew 6:24]. ¶This monster has a stone in its eye called 'hyenia' which, if someone puts it under his tongue, enables him to foretell the future. An animal that the hyena has looked at three times cannot move. It is said to be very cunning. In Ethiopia it mates with lions, and a monster called a 'crocote' results: this too makes human sounds. It never moves from its chosen territory, but is always found in the same place. It has no gums in its mouth. It has only one tooth which never changes and is covered with a kind of capsule so that it does not get damaged.

¶In Asia there is an animal called the bonnacon

which has a bull's head and body, except for the mane of a horse. But its horns wind back on themselves in such a way that anyone who falls on them is not wounded. The protection which is denied to this monster through its horns is provided by its belly. When it flees, the excrement from the stomach of the beast produces such a stench over an area of two acres that its heat singes everything it touches. By this poisonous dung it keeps all pursuers at bay.

¶Apes are so called because they ape the behaviour of rational human beings. They are very conscious of the elements, and are cheerful when the moon is new, and sad when it wanes. Their nature is such

that if a mother bears twins, she will love one and
hate the other. If she happens to be pursued by hunters, she will clasp the one she loves in front of her and carry the one she hates on her back. But when she is weary of running upright, she willingly drops the one she loves, and unwillingly carries the one she hates on her back. Apes have no tails. ¶The devil has the same form, with a head but no tail. If the whole of the ape is hateful, his backside is even more horrible and disgusting. The devil was at first one of the angels in heaven, but he was a hypocrite and deceitful and lost his tail: in the end he will be overcome, as the Apostle says: 'The Lord shall consume him with the spirit of his mouth' [II Thessalonians 2:8]. ¶'Simia', the Latin word for apes, comes from the Greek and means 'with nostrils pressed together'. Their nostrils are indeed pressed together, and their faces are horrible, with folds, like a disgusting pair of bellows; she-goats have the same nostrils. Monkeys have tails, but that is the only difference between them and apes. There are also baboons, which are very common in Ethiopia. They can make great leaps, and their bite is severe. They can never be properly tamed, and always remain rather wild. Sphinxes are also a kind of ape, with shaggy upper arms; they can be taught to forget their wild nature.

¶There are also creatures called satyrs, with almost pleasing faces and strange, restless gestures. They are hairy almost all over, and are different from the others. They have beards and broad tails. They are not difficult to catch, but difficult to keep alive. They can only live under their native Ethiopian sky.

¶The Latin name for deer, 'cervi', comes from the
Greek 'ceraton', horns. Stags are the enemies of
serpents: as soon as they feel the symptoms of illness,
they entice snakes out of their holes with the breath
of their noses, and overcoming their harmful poison,
feed on them and are cured. They also eat a herb
called dittany, and by doing so draw out arrows
which have wounded them. They are entranced by
the whistling of a pan-pipe; they can hear anything
with pricked ears, but nothing if they lay their ears
back. Deer by nature like to change their homeland,
and for this reason seek new pastures, helping each
other on the journey. If they have to cross a great
river or lake on the way, they place their heads on
the hindquarters of the deer in front, and, in following each other, do not feel hindered by their weight.
And if they come to a place where they might get
dirty, they jump rapidly across it. Another peculiar-
ity of their nature is that after they have eaten a
snake, they hasten to a spring and, drinking from it,
their grey hairs and all signs of old age vanish. ¶The
nature of deer is like that of the members of Holy
Church who leave this homeland (that is, the world)
because they prefer the new pastures of heaven,
and support each other on the way; those who are
more perfect help their lesser brethren through their

example and good works, and support them. If they find a place of sin, they spring over it at once, and if the devil enters their body after they have committed a sin, they hasten to Christ, the spring of truth, and confess, drinking in His commandments, and are renewed, laying aside their old guilt. Stags rage wildly with desire as soon as the appointed time for mating inflames them with lust. Does do not conceive until Arcturus appears in the heavens, even if they have mated before this. They do not raise their young at random in the open, but with loving care they hide them, and, concealed among the depths of foliage and grasses, they make them stay in hiding by striking them with their feet. As soon as the young are strong enough to flee, they teach them to run by exercising them, and accustom them to leap over huge chasms. If they hear the barking of hounds, they run with the wind, so that their scent is carried away with them. They are readily startled, and thus make an easy target for archers. The right horn yields better medicine than the left. If you want to make snakes flee, you can burn either of them. Their teeth indicate their age; an old stag has few or none. Alexander the Great put collars on stags to discover how long they lived; a century after they had been captured, they showed no signs of old age.

¶The word 'tragelaphus' comes from the Greek; although they are of the same kind as stags, they have hairy forequarters like he-goats, and luxuriant beards on their chins. They are only found near the River Phasis on the Black Sea. Fawns are the young of deer. They flee instantly, and are timid and gentle creatures. Martial says of them: 'The boar is feared for his tusks; horns defend the stag; but what are harmless deer but prey?' These animals signify either Christ or innocent men. The bride says of the bridegroom in the Song of Songs: 'My beloved is like a roe, or a young hart' [2:9]. Christ is therefore like a roe in His humility, when He was made flesh, and like a fawn born of deer, that is of the patriarchs,

from whom He was descended in the flesh, in the variety of His virtues and in His innocence.

¶The goat is called in Latin 'caper', because it captures rough places. Others say the Latin name comes from 'crepitus', a rustling noise. These are the tame goats, which the Greeks called gazelles because they had such keen sight. They dwell in the heights of the hills and when they see men a long way off, they can tell whether they are hunters or travellers. In the same way Christ loved the high hills, that is the prophets and Apostles, as the Song of Songs says:

'Behold, He cometh leaping upon the mountains,
skipping upon the hills' [2:8]. Our Lord refreshes
Himself in the Church; the good works of Christians
are the food of Him who said: 'For I was anhungered,
and ye gave me meat; I was thirsty, and ye gave me
drink' [Matthew 25:35]. The valleys between the
high hills are the Church, in divers places in Scripture. In the Song of Songs: 'My beloved is like a kid,
or a young hart' [2:9]. The very keen sight of the
goat, by which it can discern things afar off, signifies
our Lord who is God the all-knowing Lord and God.
Elsewhere it is written: 'The Lord looketh from
heaven; He beholdeth all the sons of men. From
the place of His habitation He looketh upon all
the inhabitants of the earth. He fashioneth their
hearts alike; He considereth all their works.' [Psalm
33:13-16]. Finally, just as the goat recognises the
arrival of the hunters from a distance, so Christ saw
through the wiles of those who betrayed Him and
said: 'Behold, he is at hand that doth betray me'
[Matthew 26:46].

¶The wild goat grazes in higher and higher pasture, searching out the good plants from the harmful ones with sharp eyes, and grazes on these. If it is wounded, it searches out the herb dittany and is cured by touching it. In the same way, good preachers graze in the law of our Lord and delight in good works as in sustenance, always growing in virtue. They distinguish good principles from evil ones with the eyes of the heart, and ruminate on those they have chosen; they study good and commit to memory the best principles. If they are wounded by sin, they run to Christ, confessing their sins, and are quickly healed. Christ is truly likened to dittany; for just as dittany expels iron

from a wound and heals it, so Christ drives out
the devil through confession and forgives the sin.

¶The monoceros is a monster with a horrible bray; it has the body of a horse, the feet of an elephant and a tail like that of a stag. A horn of extraordinary splendour projects from the middle of its forehead, four feet in length, and so sharp that anything it strikes is easily pierced by the blow. It is never taken into the power of human beings while it lives; it can be killed but never captured alive.

¶The bear gets its Latin name 'ursus' because it shapes its cubs with its mouth, from the Latin word 'orsus'. For they are said to give birth to shapeless lumps of flesh, which the mother licks into shape. The bear's tongue forms the young which it brings forth. But this is because they are born before they are mature: the birth is only thirty days after conception, and this hasty fertility creates unformed young. The bear's head is weak, and its greatest power is in its arms and loins; for this reason they

often walk upright. They do not neglect the healing
arts: if they are seriously injured and afflicted with
wounds, they know how to heal themselves by
applying mullein to their sores, which heals them as
soon as it touches them. A sick bear will eat ants.
The bears in Numidia have longer hair than any
others. They mate in the same way wherever they
are found, not in the fashion of other four-footed
beasts, but embracing each other in human fashion.
Winter awakes their desire. The males respect the
pregnant females, and if they live in the same cave,
they occupy separate lairs. The time of childbirth is
accelerated with them, because the womb is freed of
its burden after thirty days. And this rapid pregnancy produces formless creatures. They give birth
to little formless lumps of flesh, white in colour and
without eyes. They shape them by gradually licking
them with their tongue, warming them in the
meanwhile on their breast, so that the heat of the
embrace brings them to life. They eat no food during
this time, at least not during the first fortnight. The
males fall into such a deep sleep that they do not
even wake if they are wounded, and the females stay
in hiding for three months after the birth. When
they emerge into the daylight they find the light so
harsh that you would think they had been blinded.

¶They love to attack beehives, and are very partial to honeycombs, since there is nothing they like to eat so much as honey. If they eat the apples of the mandrake plant, they must die, but they counter this mortal danger by swallowing ants in order to recover their health. If they attack bulls, they know just where to wound them, and concentrate on the horns and the nostrils, because the nostrils are very tender and the pain is all the greater. The bear signifies the devil, ravager of the flocks of our Lord, and unjust rulers; in the book of Kings, the boys who taunted Elisha were eaten by two bears who came out of the woods; they signify the two Roman emperors, Vespasian and Titus, who devoured the Jews who taunted our Saviour and crucified Him on Calvary. Also, 'The lion and the bear shall come and take the ram from the flock' [I Samuel 17:34].

¶In India there is a beast called leucrota, swifter than all other wild beasts. It is as big as an ass; it has the hindquarters of a stag, the chest and legs of a lion, the head of a horse and cloven hooves. Its mouth stretches from ear to ear. Instead of teeth it has a continuous bone. So much for its shape; with its voice it imitates the sound of speech.

¶The crocodile is so called from the colour of crocuses. They live in the River Nile, four-footed animals equally at home on land or in the water and more than twenty cubits long. The crocodile is armed with monstrous teeth and claws and has such a tough skin that however hard you throw a stone at it, it will not hurt the beast. It goes into the water at night and rests by day on the land. It lays its eggs on land, and both male and female take it in turns to hatch them. A certain kind of fish whose serrated spines tear open the soft part of their belly kills them. Alone among animals they can move their upper jaw and hold the lower one still. From their dung is made an ointment with which old women and faded whores anoint their faces, and appear beautiful until their sweat washes it off. ¶The crocodile represents the hypocrite or luxurious liver and miser, who, although he is puffed up with the froth of pride, spotted with the corruption of luxury and beset by the sickness of avarice, nonetheless makes himself appear strict and without fault in upholding the laws in men's sight. The crocodile lives at night in the water and by day on the land; although the hypocrites live a depraved life, they nonetheless enjoy the reputation of a holy and up-right life. They move the upper part of their mouths, because they present to others the teachings of the Holy Father, while by no means practising what they preach. Their dung is used as an ointment:

the wicked are often praised by inexperienced men,
and this praise is like a salve which makes their
misdeeds heroic acts. When the just judge is moved
in his wrath to strike them for their evil deeds, then
all the splendour of this praise vanishes like smoke.

¶In India there is a beast called the manticore.
It has a triple row of teeth, the face of a man, and
grey eyes; it is blood-red in colour and has a lion's
body, a pointed tail with a sting like that of a
scorpion, and a hissing voice. It delights in eating
human flesh. Its feet are very powerful and it can

jump so well that neither the largest of ditches nor the broadest of obstacles can keep it in.

¶Ethiopia is the home of a creature called the parander, as large as an ox, with the footprints of an ibis, branching horns, the head of a stag, the colouring of a bear and the same thick pelt. They say that the parander can change its shape when it is frightened, and if it conceals itself it becomes like whatever it is near, whether it is a white stone or green foliage, or whatever else it may happen to be.

¶The fox has very supple feet and never runs in a straight line but always in devious ways. It is a clever, cheating animal. If it is hungry and cannot find anything to eat, it rolls in red earth, so that it seems as if it is spotted with blood, and lies on the ground holding its breath, so that it is hardly breathing. The birds see that it is not breathing, and is lying there spotted with blood with its tongue hanging out, and think it is dead. They fly down to perch on it, and it seizes them and devours them. The fox is the symbol of the devil, who appears to be dead to all living things until he has them by the throat and punishes them. But for holy men he is truly dead, reduced to nothing by faith. Those who wish to do

66 his deeds shall die, as the Apostle says: 'For if ye live after the flesh, ye shall die; but if ye through the spirit do mortify the deeds of the body, ye shall live' [Romans 8:13]. David says: 'They shall go into the lower parts of the earth; they shall fall by the sword; they shall be a portion for foxes' [Psalm 63:10].

¶The hare (lepus) is called light-footed (levipes) because it runs so swiftly. It is a swift creature, and fairly timid. The hare represents men who fear God, and who put their trust not in themselves but in the Creator. So we read Solomon's words: 'The hares are but a feeble folk, yet make they their houses in the rocks' [Proverbs 30:26]. Whence the Psalmist says: 'The high hills are a refuge for the hedgehogs; and the rocks for the hares' [104:18].

For the rock is Christ. It is written of Moses that he,
the hare of the Lord, shall stand in the cleft of the
rock, because he hoped for salvation through the
passion of our Redeemer. The hedgehog is a very
timid animal, but always provided by nature with
armour: its skin is covered with very thick, sharp
bristles. But it does not rely only on its natural
armour; lest any harm should come to it it always
hides among the stones. It may fairly be likened to
the man who, fearing to be judged for his sins,
knows that he has a firm refuge in the rock of Christ.

¶The chameleon is not all of one colour, but is multi-
coloured, like the pard. It is able to vary the colours
of its body very easily, whereas the bodies of other

animals cannot readily be changed in this way. The chameleon-pard is so called because while it is like the pard in having white spots, its neck is like that of a horse, its feet like those of an ox, but its head is like that of a camel. It is a native of Ethiopia.

¶There is a beast called an eale, as large as a horse, with an elephant's tail; it is black in colour and has the tusks of a wild boar as well as exceptionally long horns which are adapted to every kind of move-ment. For they are not rigid but can be moved as needed when it fights. It puts one out in front in a combat, so that if it loses its tip from a blow, it can bring the other one forward.

¶The Latin word for wolf comes from the Greek; 'lupus' in Latin is 'likos' in Greek, which derives from their word for biting, because wolves kill everything they find when they are ravenous. Others say that the word comes from the Greek 'leopos', lion-footed, because, as with lions, their strength is in their feet. Nothing on which they trample can survive. Just as the wolf gets its name from its rapacity, so we call whores 'she-wolves', because they destroy the wealth of their lovers. The wolf is a ravenous beast, and thirsts for blood. Its strength is in its chest and muzzle, not in its legs. It cannot bend its neck backwards. It is said to live sometimes on prey, sometimes on earth, and occasionally on wind. The she-wolf only bears cubs in May, when it thunders. Its cunning is such that it does not catch prey near to its lair to feed its young, but fetches it from afar off. If it has to hunt its prey by night, it slinks up to the sheepfold like a lame dog, and, so that the dogs do not catch its scent and wake the shepherds, it goes upwind. And if a twig breaks under its foot and makes a noise, it punishes that foot by biting it. Its eyes shine in the night like lanterns; its nature is such that if it sees a man before the man catches sight of it, it can deprive him of his voice, and it will then take no notice of him because it has won this victory over his voice. Equally, if the wolf thinks that it has been seen first, it loses its wildness and cannot run away. Solinus, who tells us much about the nature of things, says that there is a little patch of hair on its tail which is a love-charm: if the wolf is afraid that it will be caught, it tears it off with its teeth of its own accord. The hair has no effect if it is not taken from the wolf while it is still alive. The wolf is the devil, who is always envious of mankind, and continually prowls round the sheepfolds of the Church's believers, to kill their souls and to corrupt them. The fact that it only gives birth in May when it thunders reminds us of the devil, who fell from heaven in the first flush of his pride. And the wolf's

strength in its forequarters and weakness in its
hindquarters remind us that the devil was at first
an angel in heaven, but then turned apostate. Its
eyes shine in the night like lanterns because many of
the devil's works seem to blind and foolish men like
beautiful and wholesome deeds. ¶The wolf only
mates on twelve days in each year. They can bear
hunger for a long time, and after a lengthy fast they
will devour a huge meal. Ethiopia produces wolves
with coloured manes, so varied that no colour is
missing from them. The Ethiopian wolves can jump
so high that they can move as quickly in a series of
jumps as if they were running. They never attack
men. In winter they are hairy, but in summer they
are naked. The Ethiopians call them 'theas'.

¶The dog may get its Latin name, 'canis', from the Greek 'cenos'. It is believed that this name comes from the sound (canore) of its barking: when it does this, it is also said to sing (canere). There is no creature cleverer than the dog; they have more understanding than any other beast. They also know their name and love their master. Dogs are of various kinds; some track wild beasts in the forests, others guard flocks of sheep from the attacks of wolves, others guard the houses and wealth of their master, lest they are robbed at night by thieves, and will lay down their lives for their master. They go willingly to hunt with him and will guard his dead body, never leaving it. In short, their nature is such that they cannot live without human company.

¶We read how dogs love their masters very greatly, as in the case of King Garamantes, who was captured by his enemies and led into captivity; but two hundred hounds forced their way in a body through the enemy line and brought him back, resisting all opposition. When Jason was killed, his dog refused all food, and died of hunger. The dog of King Lysimachus hurled itself into the flames when its master's funeral pyre was lit. When a dog could not be separated from its condemned master in the days of the consul Apius Iunius Pictimus, it accompanied him to prison, and when he was executed soon afterwards it followed him to the scaffold, barking loudly. The people of Rome took pity on it, and gave it food, but it took the food to its master's mouth. Finally the corpse was thrown into the Tiber, and the dog tried to bring it ashore. If a dog follows the track of a hare or a stag and comes to where the paths divide or to a crossroads, he will look silently at the ways, and will decide rationally on the evidence of his keen sense of smell. Either the animal went this way, he says to himself, or that way, or it hid in this rocky cleft. But I know that it did not go in these directions, so it must have taken this path; by rejecting false trails he arrives at the truth.

¶After a murder has been committed, dogs have often provided persuasive evidence which has led to the conviction of the criminal, and their silent testimony can usually be believed. There is a story that in a remote quarter of Antioch a man who had a dog with him was murdered in the evening twilight by a soldier intent on robbery. Under cover of darkness, he fled elsewhere. The body lay unburied, and a crowd of spectators gathered. The dog howled by its side, lamenting his master's fate. The soldier, cunningly thinking that by mingling with the crowd and appearing confident he would prove his innocence, approached the corpse as if he was showing his sympathy for the dead man. The dog ceased to howl for a moment and sought his revenge, seized the man and took up his dirge again, moving all who saw it to tears. And because he fastened on this man alone among many, he proved his case, because in the end the soldier was bewildered by such a clear proof, and could not argue that he had been accused out of hate, enmity or envy. So he had to confess his crime and submit to punishment because he could think of nothing to say in his defence. ¶A dog's tongue will heal a wound if he licks it. His way of life is temperate. The tongues of puppies are a very good cure for wounds of the intestines. A dog's nature is such that it returns to its vomit and eats it again. If a dog swims across a river and has meat or something else in its mouth, he will open his mouth if he sees its shadow, and by trying to seize this imaginary piece of meat loses the real one that he is carrying. In such ways, the dogs are like the preachers who by warnings and by righteous living turn aside the ambushes of the devil, lest he seize God's treasure, namely the souls of Christians, and carry it off. As the dog's tongue heals a wound when he licks it, so the wounds of sin are cleansed by the instruction of the priest when they are laid bare in confession. The dog's way of life is said to be moderate, as he who is set above others must be watchful in the study of wisdom and avoid all kinds of inebriation, for Sodom perished from an excess of good things. For gluttony is the way by which the devil most easily corrupts men. When the dog returns to its vomit, it signifies those who fall into sin again after they have confessed. The dog who lets go of the meat in the river because he is chasing its shadow signifies foolish men who abandon what is rightfully theirs because ambition makes them pursue the unknown. Wolf-dogs are dogs which are born of wolves and dogs, when they chance to mate. In India, bitches are tied up at night in the forests, where wild tigers find them and mate with them; the result is a very swift dog which is so strong that it can pull down lions and overcome them.

¶The sheep is a soft animal with wool, a defenceless body, and a peaceful nature; it gets its Latin name, 'ovis', from oblations or offerings, because the men of old when they first made sacrifices did not slaughter bulls but sheep. Many sheep are double-toothed, having two upper teeth in addition to eight normal ones, and these were especially singled out for sacrifices by the Gentiles. At the beginning of winter the sheep eat voraciously, seizing the grass insatiably, because they feel the onset of the coming winter and are anxious to stuff themselves with food before the arrival of the frost destroys the grass. Sheep represent the innocent and simple among Christians, and the Lord Himself exhibited the mildness and patience of a sheep. Isaiah says of the death of the innocent Saviour: 'He is brought as a lamb to the slaughter, and as a sheep before her shearers is dumb, so He openeth not His mouth' [53:7]. The sheep in the Gospels are the faithful: 'The sheep hear His voice' [John 10:3]. And in the psalm: 'Thou hast put all things under his feet, all sheep and oxen, yea, and the beasts of the field' [8:6–7]. The sheep are the people of two kinds, fed by a man (that is, Christ), of whom the prophet says: 'And it shall come to pass in that day, that a man shall nourish a young cow, and two sheep, and it shall come to pass for the abundance of milk they shall give, he shall eat butter' [Isaiah 7:21–22]. Note also the wicked sheep in the Psalter: 'Like sheep they are laid in the grave, and death shall feed on them' [49:14].

¶The wether gets his Latin name 'vervex' either from 'vis', strength, because he is stronger than other sheep, or from 'vir', a man, because he is masculine; or perhaps from 'vermes', worms, because he has worms in his head which cause such itching that the wethers butt each other and charge with great force at each other. The ram (aries) is so called either after Ares, the Greek god of war, or because this was the first creature to be offered on the altars (aris) of the heathen. The rams signify the Apostles or the princes of the Church. We read in Isaiah: 'The rams of Nabaioth shall minister unto thee' [60:7], and in the Psalms: 'Bring unto the Lord the offspring of rams'. For the princes of the Church, like the leaders of the flock, shall lead the Christian people in the ways of the Lord. And we are told to offer the offspring of rams because such men are the result of the preaching of the Apostles, not of some stranger who experiments with wicked teachings. Rams are like the Apostles because these animals have powerful foreheads and always over-throw whatever they strike. The Apostles did the same with their preaching, breaking down various superstitious and well-established idols with the heavenly word. Elsewhere, however, the rams represent wicked rulers, as in Ezekiel: 'Arabia, and all the princes of Kedar, they occupied with thee in lambs, and rams, and goats' [27:21].

¶The lamb is called 'agnus' in Latin either from the Greek word for pious, or from 'agnoscere', to recognise, because above all other animals it is able to recognise its mother, so much so that if it is in the

middle of a large flock, as soon as its mother bleats, it
recognises its parent's voice and hastens to it, seeking for the familiar source of its mother's milk. And the mother will pick out her lamb among many thousands of others. Their bleating appears to be the same, and they look alike, but nonetheless the mother can pick out her offspring from the rest, and will treat only this one with motherly care. The lamb is a symbol of the person of our mystic Saviour, whose innocent death saved mankind, as John says: 'Behold the Lamb of God, who taketh away the sins of the world' [1:36]. The lamb is also any one among the faithful whose life is blameless, and who obeys his mother the Church, recognising her voice and coming to her side and obeying her commandments. Lambs are blessed in the Gospel: 'Feed my lambs' [John 21:15].

¶Young kids are very fat and taste excellent; so their Latin name 'edus' is related to eating (edere). They represent the sinners, who shall stand on the left hand of God on the Day of Judgement, in the same way that the just, represented by sheep, shall stand on His right hand. It is truly said in the Gospel: 'He shall set the sheep on His right hand, but the goats on the left' [Matthew 25:33]. But sometimes the just are called by this name, when they have confessed their sins, as in Jeremiah: 'Remove out of the midst of Babylon, and go forth out of the land of the Chaldeans, and be as the kids among the flocks' [50:8]. Christ is like a kid because of the sins of the flesh, as in Deuteronomy: 'Thou shalt not seethe a kid in his mother's milk [14:21]. The kid can also be Antichrist: 'Yet thou never gavest me a kid, that I might make merry with my friends' [Luke 15:29].

¶The he-goat is a stubborn, lascivious animal, always eager to mate, whose eyes are so full of lust thay they look sideways, from which they get their Latin name 'hircus', for Suetonius calls the corner of the eye the 'hircus'. Its nature is so hot that diamonds, against which fire and iron are powerless, dissolve in its blood. For the he-goat, which in Jewish law was offered in atonement for sins, shows us the sinner, who in pouring out his blood (that is, in the tears of penitence) dissolves the hardness of his sins. In the Psalter, the Church says to the Lord God: 'I will offer bullocks with goats' [66:15]. The goats are the sinners or Gentiles, as in Daniel: 'Behold, an he-goat came from the west' [8:5]. The two he-goats are the two peoples, namely the Jews and the Gentiles, coming from the vine-branch of sin in Leviticus. But others have understood the two he-goats to be Christ and Barabbas. Oxen are symbols of the preachers, who successfully plough the soil of human hearts and prepare them to receive the fruitful seed of the heavenly meaning of their words. The he-goats are those who follow the depravities of the devil and clothe themselves in the shaggy hide of vice. The he-goat is 'hircus' in Latin, akin to 'hirsutus', hairy; but the Church offers them with oxen when converts acknowledge Christ as their Lord.

¶The sow ('sus' in Latin) is so called because it ploughs up (subigat) its food; that is, it roots for food in the earth it has disturbed. The pig (porcus) is a filthy beast (spurcus); it sucks up filth, wallows in mud, and smears itself with slime. Horace calls the sow 'the lover of mud'. Sows signify sinners, the unclean and heretics: it is prescribed in Jewish law that the flesh of beasts with cloven hooves which do not chew the cud shall not be eaten by the faithful. The Old and New Testaments, the Law and the Gospels, support this: because heretics do not chew the cud of spiritual food, they are unclean. Sows are those who neglect their penance and return to that which they once bewailed, as Peter says in his Epistle: 'The dog is turned to his own vomit again, and the sow that was washed to her wallowing in the mire' [II Peter 2:22]. For the dog, when it vomits, casts out and puts forth the food which oppresses its breast; but when it returns to the vomit by which it had relieved itself, it burdens itself once again. Thus those who weep for the sins they have admitted put forth the iniquity of their hearts, which were sated with the evil that oppressed them inwardly. This they cast out in confession; but after confession, they begin again and take up their old ways. The sow that was washed and returns to her wallowing in the mire is filthier than before; and he who weeps for his admitted sins, but does not desist from them, earns a graver punishment, condemned by his own misdeeds which he could have prevented by repentance: and he descends as if into murky waters because he removes the cleanness of his life by such tears, which are tainted before the eyes of God. Pigs are unclean and gluttonous men in the Gospel: 'If thou cast us out, suffer us to go away into the herd of swine' [Matthew 8:31]. And again: 'Neither cast ye your pearls before swine' [Matthew 7:6]. The pig is also the man who is unclean of spirit: 'He sent him into his fields to feed swine' [Luke 15:15]. The pig can signify both the unclean and the sinners, of whom it is written in the Psalms: 'Their belly is filled with Thy hidden treasure: they are filled like swine, and leave what remains to their children' [17:14]. The Jews call those things unclean which are hidden by the Lord, in other words, those things they know to be forbidden. But the sinners shall hand over the remains of their sins to their children: 'Then answered all the people, and said, "His blood be on us, and on our children"' [Matthew 27:25]. The sow represents the sinner and luxurious liver if we understand Solomon rightly: 'As a jewel of gold in a swine's snout, so is a fair woman which is without discretion' [Proverbs 11:22]. The sow thinks on carnal things; from her thoughts wicked or wasteful deeds result, as in Isaiah: 'A people ... which eat swine flesh, and broth of abominable things is in their vessels' [65:3-4], that is, in their hearts.

¶The boar (aper) is so called from its wildness (feri-
tas), substituting a **p** for the **f**. In Greek it is called
'siagros', wild. Everything which is wild and rough
we call, derogatorily, rustic (agreste). Others say
that the boar gets its name because it lives in wild
places. The boar signifies the fierceness of the rulers
of this world. Hence the Psalmist writes of the
vineyard of the Lord: 'The boar out of the wood doth
waste it, and the wild beast of the field doth devour
it' [80:13]. He drove the Jewish people out of the
boundaries of their homeland and scattered them.
Perhaps we should acknowledge the boar to be
Vespasian, who appeared strong and cruel to them.
To call him thus implies that he was the enemy of
the Jews, who seemed to think that this animal was
unclean. The wild beast of the field reminds us of his
son Titus, who destroyed so many of the people in
the rest of the war that both the Jewish race and
their city were devoured like the grass of the field.
This vineyard (i.e. Jerusalem) had to be seized; its
walls were seen to be thrown down. In the spiritual
sense the boar means the devil because of its fierceness and strength. It is said to be a creature of the
woods because its thoughts are wild and unruly.

¶The bullock gets its Latin name 'juvencus' either because it helps (iuvat) men to till the ground, or because bullocks, never bulls, were always sacrificed to Jove by the Gentiles: the age of the beast was an important consideration. The Latin words for bull and ox, 'taurus' and 'bos', come from the Greek. The bulls in India are tawny gold in colour and as swift as birds. Their hair lies in opposite directions and they can open their mouths to the width of their head. They can turn their horns at will, and their backs are so hard that arrows simply bounce off. Their fierceness is such that if they are captured they give up the ghost. The bull is Christ. In Genesis we read: 'They have cut the sinews of the bull in their wrath'. Elsewhere bulls are the princes of this world, tossing the common people on the horns of their pride, as in Jeremiah: 'Ye bellow as bulls' [50:11], or Isaiah: 'And bulls with the princes' [34:7]. Bulls have both a good and evil significance: the good aspect is found in the Gospel: 'Behold, I have prepared my dinner: my bulls and my fatlings are killed, and all things are ready' [Matthew 22:4]. The evil aspect is reflected in the Psalms: 'The fat bulls have set about me' [22:12].

¶The ox, 'bos', is called 'boetes' in Greek. In Latin it is also called trio, because it treads on terra firma. If oxen are together they are very peaceful; they will seek out their partner under the yoke of the plough, and they will show their affection for each other by frequent lowing if they become tired. If it is about to rain they will return to their stables. If their natural senses tell them that the sky is clearing, they look out and stretch their necks out of the stable, as if to tell each other with one accord that they want to go out again. The looseness of their hide from their chin to their forequarters is called a dewlap (palearia) as if from 'pellis', skin. Oxen in scripture can mean many things; the madness of those who lead sensual lives, the strength and labours of the preachers, the humility of the Israelites. Solomon gives us an example of the first, when he is discussing the wiles of women: 'He goeth after her straightway, as an ox goeth to the slaughter' [Proverbs 7:22]. Again, the Law and Epistles use the name of the ox to describe the work of the preacher: 'Thou shalt not muzzle the ox when he treadeth out the corn' [Deuteronomy 25:4; I Corinthians 9:9].

¶Buffaloes are so called because they are similar to 'boves', oxen, but they are so wild that no yoke can be laid on them. Africa is their birthplace. The aurochs is found in Germany, with huge horns which provide the tables of kings with drinking vessels of extraordinary capacity. Aurochs and buffaloes can be seen as proud teachers and those who lord it over the people; their status is similar to that of good teachers, but they swell with pride, and trust rather in the horns of worldly power than in divine help. And against the apostolic law, they choose to rule over the clergy, rather than lead them as a flock; the Lord cursed them through the mouth of his prophet, saying: 'Woe be to the shepherds of Israel, that do feed themselves! Should not the shepherds feed the flocks? Ye eat the fat, and ye clothe you with the wool, ye kill them that are fed; but ye feed not the flock. The diseased ye have not strengthened, neither have ye healed that which was sick, neither have ye bound up that which was broken, neither have ye brought again that which was driven away, neither have ye sought that which was lost; but with force and with cruelty have ye ruled them' [Ezekiel 34:2–4].

¶The cow, 'vacca', gets its name from 'bos'; it is 'boacca', just as we have lion/lioness, a name which changes according to the sex of the creature. The cow is sometimes used in a favourable sense, as in Numbers [19:2], where it is commanded that 'a red heifer without spot, wherein is no blemish, and upon which came no yoke' shall be slain to cleanse the sanctuary of the Lord. The male usually represents strength, the female weakness. This is the case with the cow, which stands for the sacrifice of the Lord's incarnation in His weakness, of which it is written: 'For though He was crucified through weakness, yet He liveth by the power of God' [II Corinthians 13:4]. He is called a red heifer, because His human form was made red by the blood of the passion. His humanity is without blemish, all His deeds perfect; there was no spot on His human form.

¶Calves (vituli) are so called because of their green age (viridis), or because they are virgins, and have not yet borne offspring: if they had, they would be called heifers or cows. So calves belong on the good side, showing the innocence of faith, or the sincere praise of pious devotion. It is written: 'So will we render the calves of our lips' [Hosea 14:2]. And in the psalm: 'Then shall they offer calves upon thine altar' [51:19]. The writer uses calves to represent the innocent, in their first age, whose neck is a stranger to the yoke of sin; or he is prefiguring those preachers of the Gospel whose image is found in the calf which is the symbol of Luke the Evangelist, who did not make the air echo with vain bellowing, but filled the earth with the preaching of the faith of the Lord. ¶We must also think of those calves who gave up their lives as sacrifices in the sweetness of the holy altars. Augustine, the holy father, when he discusses the symbols of the Evangelists, calls the Lord Himself a calf, who offered Himself as a sacrifice for the salvation of the rest. Whether he had in mind youths, or preachers, or martyrs, the prophet could promise such calves for the altars of the Lord as he knew would be fitting for the Christian religion. Christ is the calf in the Gospel: 'Bring hither the fatted calf and kill it' [Luke 15:23]. Elsewhere in the Psalms, 'He maketh them also to skip like a calf' [29:6]. They are calves because they grow in the holy faith and their necks are free of the yoke of the law. Calves also represent the lascivious Jews, as in the psalm: 'Many calves have surrounded me, the fat bulls have attacked me' [22:12].

¶Camels get their name from their appearance, either because as soon as they are laden they seem shorter and lower and lie down ('cami' in Greek means low and short); or because camels have crooked backs and the Greek word 'camur' means crooked. There are camels in other countries, but the great majority come from Arabia. Bactria produces strong camels, but Arabia produces the greatest quantity. They differ in that the Arabian camels have a double hump and the Bactrian camels only one. They have a kind of fleshy pad on the soles of their feet, which helps to guard them from sinking in as they walk. There are two kinds of camel; one which will carry heavy loads, and a swifter kind which will only accept a light burden. They like familiar territory, and behave wildly when they want something; they go mad when it is time to mate. They hate all horses. They can put up with thirst for three days: as soon as they are able to drink, they make good their present thirst and provide for a long time into the future. They love to drink muddy water, and avoid pure water. If the water is not cloudy, they will tread in it and stir up the mud to make it dirty. They live to be a hundred years old. If they are taken into foreign lands, the change of air makes them ill. Female camels are used in war: a way was found to destroy their desire to mate, because they are much stronger if they are kept from mating. ¶The camel signifies the humility of Christ, who bears all our sins, or the Gentiles converted to the Christian faith. In the Gospel it says: 'It is easier for a camel to go through the eye of a needle, than for a rich man to enter the Kingdom of God' [Matthew 19:24], meaning that it is easier for Christ to suffer for those who are enamoured of this world than for such men to be converted to Christ. He was willing to assume the part of a camel, in taking on Himself the burdens of our weakness which he did out of humility. This is the meaning of the verse: 'The greater thou art, the more humble thyself' [Ecclesiasticus 3:18]. The needle reminds us of pricks, the pricks of pain He underwent in His passion. The eye of the needle is the straitness of Our Lord's passion, by which He in some measure rent the clothing of our nature, that is, He deemed it worthy to be put on, so that after the fall we should be remade in better fashion, rejoicing in the Apostle's words: 'For as many of you as have been baptised into Christ have put on Christ' [Galatians 3:27].

¶The ass gets its name because men sit on it (a sedendo), but this name is more fitting for horses. However, this creature carried burdens before men tamed horses, and they first tried riding on its back. It is a sluggish and senseless beast and can be captured by a man as soon as he wishes to take it. They are called Arcadian because the first large, tall asses came from Arcadia. The ass is smaller than the wild ass, but is more useful and tolerates work, not complaining even if it is badly neglected. The names ass or she-ass sometimes imply the wantonness of the lecherous, at others the gentleness of the meek, and yet elsewhere the folly of the pagans. For in spiritual terms the ass, being a brutish and

98 lecherous creature, signifies the pagan people over whom the Lord was thought worthy to preside when He entered Jerusalem, making them subject to Him, and leading them to the heavenly country, or it can mean the foolish man who follows only the pleassures of the world. Jacob says of his son Issachar: 'Issachar is a strong ass, couching down between two burdens' [Genesis 49:14]. So the pagans whom the Lord ransomed with the price of His blood were beforehand like brutish and lecherous animals, ignorant of reason. Now indeed they have become strong, subjecting the hidden things of the mind to our Saviour, and by setting their neck under the Redeemer's dominion, they bear the yoke of the teaching of the Gospel. They are made to bring tribute, offering to Christ their King the good works of faith and gifts of good things. Elsewhere, the ass represents the fool. In Deuteronomy: 'Thou shalt not plow with an ox and an ass together' [22:10], that is, do not bring the foolish man into the company of wise preachers. The ass represents the Jewish synagogue in Genesis: 'Binding . . . his ass's colt unto the choice vine' [49:11]. The firstborn of the ass represents the beginning of a life of lechery, as in Exodus: 'But the firstling of an ass shalt thou redeem with a lamb' [34:20]. Here it shows us the fool who bears

the burdens of sin and exercises the lusts of the flesh until the end of his life. Hence it is written that when Anna fed her father's asses in Essebon, she found hot springs in the desert. As the prophet says of the lustful: 'For she doted upon her paramours, whose flesh is like the flesh of asses' [Ezekiel 23:20].

¶The onager can be translated as wild ass; in Greek 'on' means ass, 'agriam' wild. They live in Africa; they are very large and untamed and wander in the desert. Single males will dominate a herd of females. The males are jealous of the newborn young, and will bite off their testicles. The mothers, aware of this, conceal them in secret places. The naturalists say that the onager brays twelve times on the night of 25 March, and the same number of times in the day; the number of hours in the day or night can be counted by the braying of the onager, which it does once an hour. This beast represents the devil, who knows how to make day and night the same, and because he sees that the people that walked in darkness have turned to God and have adhered to the belief of the righteous, he brays by day and night, and hourly seeks whom he may devour. For the onager only brays when he wants food; as Job says: 'Doth the wild ass bray when he hath grass?' [6:5]. And the Apostle says: 'Your adversary the devil, as a roaring lion, walketh about seeking whom he may devour' [I Peter 5:8].

¶The dromedary is a kind of camel, but smaller in
stature and swifter: hence his name, because the
Greeks call swiftness and running 'dromos'. It can
cover a hundred miles or more in one day. It chews
the cud like oxen, sheep and camels. The word
ruminate comes from 'rumo', the gullet, through
which food is regurgitated by animals after they
have swallowed it once.

¶Horses get their Latin name 'equi' because when
they are harnessed in a team of four, they are equally matched, in equal size, and with equal stride. The

word 'caballus' also means horse, and comes from their hollow (cavus) feet. Their hooves dig out the earth as they go, unlike other animals. They are very lively creatures, racing round the fields; they can scent battle, and the sound of the trumpet encourages them to fight, while the human voice can urge them on in a race. They are dejected when beaten, and delight in winning. Some of them can scent out enemies in battle so well that they try to bite them. Many recognise their masters, and become unmanageable if they change hands. Others will suffer no one except their master to ride them; for example, Alexander the Great had a horse named Bucephalus or Oxhead, so called either because its look was so wild, or because it had been branded like an ox on its shoulder-blade, or because two growths like ox-horns sprouted from its forehead. It was once slightly hurt by its groom and would never afterwards, if the royal saddle was put on it, allow anyone else except its lord to ride it. There are many documents which tell how it bore Alexander unharmed through the most bloody battles. Gaius Caesar's horse would only allow Caesar to ride him. When the king of the Scythians was killed in single combat and his opponent tried to strip him of his armour, his horse attacked him, kicking and biting him. When King Nicodemus was killed, his horse stopped eating and starved to death. When Antiochus conquered the Galatians, he sprang on to the horse of Cintaretus, their leader, who had been killed in the citadel; but the horse disliked the studded bit so much that he purposely slowed his pace and brought disaster on himself and his rider. With this species, the males live longer. We read of horses which lived to seventy, and a horse named Opuntes was at stud until he was forty. The desire of the mares for mating disappears if their manes are cut. When they foal, a growth appears on their foreheads, which is a love charm: it is reddish brown in colour and like a tuft of reed-grass; it is called 'hippomanes'. If the foal is taken away immediately from the mare, the mother will never offer to suckle it. The deeper they put their nostrils in the water when drinking, the hotter is their desire. If their master is killed or dies, horses will weep. It is said that only horses will weep for men, and only they feel sorrow. Centaurs share the natures of men and horses. If men go to battle, they can foretell the outcome by the eagerness (or lack of it) of their horses. The general opinion is that the ancients were right to say that a noble horse should have four qualities: form, beauty, temperament and colour.

As to form, the body should be strong and firm, the height in proportion to the animal's strength. It should have long, narrow flanks, large, well-rounded hindquarters, and broad forequarters. Its body should have thick, knotted muscles, a dry foot and a firm frog in the hoof. As for beauty, it should have a small dry head; its skin should be tight over its bones. The ears should be short and pricked, the eyes large, the nostrils wide, the neck well-arched, mane and tail thick and the hooves firm and well-rounded. Good temperament means that it should be bold, nimble on its feet, with quivering limbs which show its courage; it should be quick to rouse to swift motion from rest, and even at its fastest it should be easily reined in. The speed of a horse can be judged by its ears, its courage from the quivering of its limbs. ¶The chief colours are bay, chestnut, golden, rosy chestnut, stag-coloured, pale yellow, grey, dappled, greyish-white, white, piebald, black; then there are horses with mixed colours, such as bay and black. Horses with other colour mixtures and ash-grey horses should be avoided. In ancient times cart-horses (veredos) were so called because they pulled four-wheeled wagons (veherent redas), or because they went on the public roads, 'vias', on which such wagons were driven.

¶The name mule comes from the Greek, because the beast is yoked by the miller to the heavy millstone and forced to walk round it to turn the mill. The Jews say that Ana, a great-nephew of Esau, first had mares mounted by asses in the desert, and that mules arose in this unnatural fashion. Wild asses were also mated to she-asses, and their offspring were remarkably swift. Human ingenuity has brought various kinds of animals together, and produced a new species by this unnatural mixture, just as Jacob unnaturally tried to obtain the same colouring by breeding. For his sheep conceived lambs of the same colour as the ram appeared to them when they saw it reflected in the water as they mated. Finally it is said that the same happens with mares: if they see noble stallions as they conceive, their foals will be like them. Pigeon fanciers also try to place images of beautiful pigeons where pigeons mate, so that, enchanted by the sight of them, they will produce similar offspring. For the same reason, many people think that pregnant women should not look at ugly beasts such as apes and monkeys, in case they should bring children into the world who resemble these caricatures. For women's nature is such that they produce offspring according to the image they see or have in mind at the moment of ecstasy as they conceive. In mating, animals transmit the forms that they see outwardly to their inward parts, and so make their appearance their own. Among the beasts, those which come from parents of different species are called mules if they are from horses and she-asses, hybrids from wild boar and domestic sow, tyrius from sheep and he-goat, and musimo from she-goat and ram. The last is the leader of the flock. The licissa comes from a wolf and a tame bitch. ¶The mule, because it is a beast of burden, represents those who follow foolish ways, like Absalom, who rode a mule and raised a rebellion against his father, and was later pursued and justly killed. The Psalmist warns his hearers with these words: 'Be ye not as the horse or as the mule which

have no understanding: whose mouth must be held
in with bit and bridle, lest they come near unto thee'
[32:9]. For he wishes to prevent men of this kind
from being taken up with the wiles of the devil and
weighted down with the burden of vice, lest by
wrongly obeying their pride they should be utterly
condemned. But what does he tell such men to do? It
is not other than the kind of command given to
dumb animals; by such comparisons he compels the
fool to acknowledge the truth. For when he said
'with a bridle', he is speaking of horses: 'frenum', a
bridle, is so called because it is used to restrain wild
animals (fera), and the ancients called the horse a
wild animal. 'With a bit' refers to the mule, and
these bonds restrain the beasts we have mentioned,
so that they go where their master wishes and do
not wander at will. The jaws are the means by
which animals chew their food and keep themselves
alive, and the Psalmist is saying that the very jaws
of the disobedient should be restrained, their food
should be rationed, so that, compelled by fasting,
they will yield to the rule of their Creator.

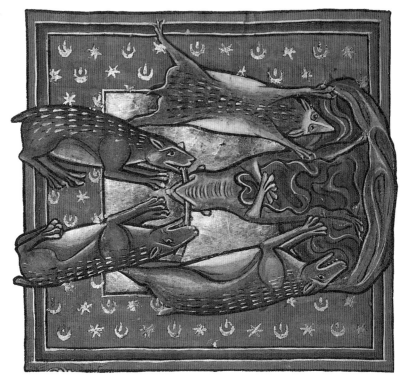

¶There is an animal called the badger which is also known as the melot. It bites and is unclean, inhabiting mountains and rocky places. It makes holes underground by scraping and digging with its feet. Some badgers are born to be servants to the others. They lie on their backs and pile on their bellies soil which the others have dug out. Then they hold a piece of wood in their mouth and clutch the soil with their four feet. The others sink their teeth into the wood and drag them backwards out of the holes, to the astonishment of anyone who sees it.

¶This creature is called mouser because she kills mice. The common word is cat because she captures them. They have such sharp sight that the brightness of their glance overcomes the darkness of night. 'Catus' is the Greek word for cunning.

¶The mouse is a feeble little creature, which gets its name because mice are born from the dampness of the earth; the mouse

comes from the humus. Their liver grows at the full moon, like some sea creatures, and diminishes as the moon wanes. The shrew (sorex) gets its Latin name because it gnaws and cuts like a saw (serra). Mice represent greedy men who seek earthly goods, and make the goods of others their prey.

¶The weasel, 'mustela', is a sort of long mouse; 'telon' means long in Greek. It is very cunning; when it gives birth to its young in a house,  it carries them from one place to another and puts them somewhere different each time. It attacks serpents and mice. There are two kinds of weasel: one lives in the woods and is rather bigger – the Greeks call them 'ictidas' – and the other lives in houses. Some people say that they conceive through their ear and give birth through their mouth, and others that it is the opposite way round, that they conceive through their mouth and give birth through their ear. They are said to be skilled in healing, so that if they find that their young have been killed, they can bring them to life again. They signify those men who readily listen to the seed of the divine word but, held back by the love of worldly things, neglect it and do not want to know more about what they have heard. The weasel signifies a thief, as in Leviticus.

 ¶The mole is so called because it is condemned to perpetual darkness because of its blindness. It has no eyes, always digs the earth

and turns it over, and eats the roots. The mole, condemned to perpetual blindness, is the image of pagan idols, blind, deaf and dumb; or even their worshippers, wandering in the eternal darkness of ignorance and folly. Isaiah writes of them: 'In that day a man shall cast his idols . . . to the moles, and to the bats' [2:20], that is, the blind shall worship the blind. The mole is also the symbol of heretics or false Christians who, like the eyeless mole which digs in the earth, heaping up the soil and eating the roots beneath the crops, lack the light of true knowledge and devote themselves to earthly deeds. They serve the desires of the flesh zealously, and succumb to the lure of pleasure, while they try in every way possible to gnaw at the roots of all that is good.

¶The dormouse (glis) is so called because sleep makes it fat; 'gliscere' means to grow. They sleep all winter, and lie motionless, as if dead. In the summer-  time, they come to life again. They signify those who are rendered useless by the sluggishness of sloth and do not want to work usefully. It is written of such men: 'The sluggard will not plow by reason of the cold; therefore shall he beg in harvest and have nothing' [Proverbs 20:4], for the person who is now idle and inactive in earthly life will beg in vain at the Judgement Day, when the harvest is gathered in. Such a man cannot share with the just in the joys of heavenly life.

¶The hedgehog is an animal which is covered in spines. It gets its name because it curls up when it closes itself in its spikes, which are the defence which protects it from its enemies. For as soon as it senses danger, it curls up and rolls into a ball and retreats behind its armour. It is quite clever: if it picks a grape off the vine, it rolls on it and spears it with its spines in order to carry it home to its young. It is also called 'echinus'; this creature has the foresight to equip its den with two holes for ventilation. When it notices that the north wind has started to blow, it blocks the north entrance; as soon as it notices that the south wind drives the mists into the air it goes to the north entrance to avoid the wind from this direction, which comes from dangerous lands. For in mystical terms the hedgehog is a sinner full of vices like spines, skilled in wicked cunning, and in deceits and robberies. He cheats others of the fruits of their labours and takes their food for himself. Of them it is written: 'There shall the hedgehog make her nest and nourish her young' [Isaiah 34:15]. In the Psalms we find that 'the rocks are the refuge of the hedgehog'. It is the most timid of animals, always bearing the armour provided for it by nature: very sharp and densely packed bristles, like stakes, fortify its hide. But it does not trust solely to its native defence; so that it cannot be seized by a trick, it hides among the rocks. It is like the man bristling with sins, who fears the judgement to come, and takes very secure refuge in the rock of Christ.

¶The ant (formica) is so called because it carries grains (micas) of spelt: it is a very shrewd creature. It thinks of the future, and prepares its provisions for winter in the summer. At harvest time it seeks out wheat, and will not touch barley; if it rains on the grain it has stored, the ant will throw it all out. They say that in Ethiopia there are ants in the shape of dogs, which root out grains of gold with their feet and guard them so that no one can steal them. If they detect a thief, they hound him to death. The ant has three habits. The first habit is that they march in order, each carrying a grain of corn in its mouth. Those who have no corn do not say to the others, 'Give me your grain,' but follow the tracks of those who have gone out earlier until they find corn, and then they take it to their nest. This should be a good reminder of clever men, who collect like the ants in order to receive their reward in the future. Its second habit is that when it stores grain in its nest, it divides the store in two, in case the winter rains soak it and make it germinate, so that the ant dies of hunger. In

the same way you, O men, should keep the word of
the Old and New Testaments separate, that is, distinguish between the carnal and the spiritual, lest
the letter kill you: for the Law is spiritual, as the
Apostle says: 'For the letter killeth, but the spirit
giveth life' [II Corinthians 3:6]. For the Jews paid
attention only to the letter of the Law and ignored
its spiritual meaning; therefore they perished of
hunger. The third habit of the ant is this: at harvest
time it wanders through the cornfields, and tests the
blades with its mouth, to see if they are barley or
wheat. If it is barley, it goes to another blade and
smells it, and if it finds that it is wheat, it climbs up
the stalk, takes the corn and carries it home. Barley
is food for ordinary animals. Hence Job's saying:
'Barley grew for me instead of wheat' [31:40], that
is, the teachings of heretics, for these are only barley
and you should keep them far from you, because
they corrupt men's souls and destroy them. O Christian, flee from all heretics, whose teachings are false
and enemies of the truth. For the Holy Scripture
says: 'Go to the ant, thou sluggard; consider her
ways and be wise' [Proverbs 6:6]. For the ant has
never been taught, and has no one to command it,
and no master to teach it how to find food. It gathers
its harvest from your labours; while you often go

hungry, it is never in need. It has no locked chests, no impregnable guard, no unapproachable fortress. The watchman has to look on as thieves break in, and dare not stop them; the owner suffers harm, without being able to revenge himself. Their booty is carried in a dark procession across the fields, the paths teem with their comings and goings, and what they do not carry in their little mouths they load on to their backs. The ant knows how to use fine weather. If it sees that its corn is damp or wet from rain, it scents the air to see if mild weather can be expected; if it is, then it opens its storehouse and carries the grain outside on its shoulders, so that the corn can dry out in the sunshine.

¶Frogs are so called from their chattering, because they croak among the marshes where they are born, and utter harsh cries  with their voices. In the Apocalypse, frogs represent demons: 'And I saw three unclean spirits like frogs come out of the mouth of the dragon' [Revelation 16:13]. For frogs signify the heretics and their demons who linger at the banquet of the decadent senses, and do not cease to utter their vain chatter.

¶There is an animal called the dea, in Greek 'salamander' or 'stellio' in Latin. It is a small feeble creature, of which Solomon says: 'The salamander is in kings' palaces' [Proverbs 30:28]. The naturalists say of it that if it falls by chance in the glowing coals in the grate, or in the fire beneath the furnace, or into any other fire, it at once puts it out. They are as marvellous to all men as Ananias, Azarias and Misael (Shadrach, Meshach and Abednego), who were put in the burning fiery furnace, and the flames did not touch them: Daniel declares that they came forth untouched and unblemished from the fire. Elsewhere it is said of salamanders that they stop up the mouths of lions, and put an end to the rule of fire. And whoever believes in the Lord with his whole heart, and perseveres in good works, shall go through the fire of Gehenna, and the flames shall not touch him: the prophet Isaiah says: 'Thou shalt go through the fire and it shall not burn thee'.

¶The eagle is so called because it is eagle-eyed. Its sight is so sharp that it can glide over the sea, beyond the ken of human eyes; from so great a height it can see the fish swimming in the sea. It will plunge down

like a thunderbolt and seize its prey, and bring it
ashore. When it grows old, its wings grow heavy and its eyes cloud over. Then it seeks out a fountain and flies up into the atmosphere of the sun; there its wings catch fire and the darkness of its eyes is burnt away in the sun's rays. It falls into the fountain and dives under water three times: at once its wings are restored to their full strength and its eyes to their former brightness. ¶So you, O man, whose clothes are old and the eyes of whose heart are darkened, should seek out the spiritual fountain of the Lord, and lift the eyes of your mind to God, who is the fount of justice; and then you will renew your youth like the eagle. It is also said of the eagle that it tests its young by putting them into the sun's rays while it holds them in its claws in mid-air. In this way the young eagle which looks fearlessly at the sun without harming its eyesight proves that it is the true offspring of its race. If it looks away, however, it is at once dropped, because it is a creature unworthy of so great a father: just as it was unworthy of being carried up, so it is unworthy of being reared. The eagle carries out the sentence without any bitterness in its nature, but as an impartial judge. He does not turn from his own young, but refuses to accept a stranger.

¶In Ireland there are many birds called barnacles, which nature produces in a way which contradicts her own laws. They are like marsh geese, but smaller. They first appear as growths on pine-logs floating on the water. Then they hang from seaweed on the log, their bodies protected by a shell so that they may grow more freely; they hold on by their beaks. In due course they grow a covering of strong feathers and either fall into the water or change to free flight in the air. They take their food from the sap of the wood and from the sea in a mysterious way as they grow. I have seen them myself, with my own eyes, many times: thousands of these small birdlike bodies hanging from just one log on the seashore, in their shells and already formed. When they mate, they do not lay eggs, and no bird of this kind ever sits on eggs to hatch them. You will never have seen them anywhere on the land, breeding or building nests. For this reason, in some parts of Ireland, bishops and men of religion eat them during times of fasting without committing a sin, because they are neither flesh, nor born of flesh. ¶Pause, O unhappy few, pause even if it is too late. You do not dare to deny, because you respect the law of the Old Testament, that the first man was born of clay, without male or female parents, and that the second was born of the male without a female parent. Only the third, born in the usual way from male and female, can you in your stiff-necked thinking approve and affirm. But the fourth generation, in which salvation was born of a woman alone, who had not known a man, you hate, to your own down-fall, because you are obstinate in your malice. Blush, wretched man, blush! Look at the example of nature, which daily creates and brings forth new creatures without male or female help to instruct us and confirm us in the faith. The first generation came from clay, the latest from wood. The first, which only happened once because it was the doing of the Lord of nature, will always be a mystery. The present example is just as wonderful, but is less mysterious, because nature imitates itself and repeats the process. For human nature is such that only what is unusual or rare seems worthy of admiration.

¶There are many birds here [in Ireland] whose nature is of two kinds; they are called ospreys. They are smaller than an eagle, but larger than a hawk. One of their feet is equipped with talons, open and ready to seize prey, while the other is closed and peaceful, suited only to swimming. It is an amazing example of nature's playful ways. There is something remarkable about these birds, which I have often seen with my own eyes. They fly high above the sea so that they can fasten their gaze on the depths below, and move their wings gently so that they stay in the same place. When they see fish hiding in the depths of the sea, using their keen sight to penetrate the turbulence of air and water, they plunge down with extraordinary speed. When they dive into the waves and rise out of them again, they use their swimming foot to control their movement, seizing their prey with their talons, in which they carry it off. So the ancient enemy of mankind sees with his sharp intellect whatever we do in the turbulent waves of this world; and while he seems to approach us on a peaceful footing through success in worldly things, he nonetheless seizes and destroys our soul with grasping talons, bloody with prey.

¶There are in Ireland many small birds called waterouzels (martinetas), which are smaller than blackbirds. Here they are common, but elsewhere they are rare; they live on river banks, and look rather like quail, and they dive into the water to catch the little fish on which they live. While in all other respects they are like others of their species, the water-ouzels in Ireland are a different colour, having a black and white belly; the rest of them is like a parrot or peacock with brilliant green colouring. They are very conspicuous and beautiful. If, after they have died, they are kept in a dry place, they never putrefy. If they are put among clothes or anything else they preserve them from moths and give them a pleasant scent. And, what is even more extraordinary, if they are hung by the beak in a dry place, they renew their plumage each year, as if some part of the living spirit was dormant in the remains. So holy men, dead to the world but alight with the flame of love, and, as it were, placed in a dry place, take on a kind of incorruptibility and preserve themselves, and those associated with them, from the mouth of vice, making themselves praiseworthy by the good scent of their virtues. ¶And while they hang in the sublime world by concentrating their minds on higher things, they are daily renewed and improved by throwing off their old habits and growing in their new virtues. They put off the old Adam entirely, and put on the new man.

¶There is a bird called the coot, which the Greeks call 'fene', which takes up the rejected chicks of the eagle, which the eagle will not acknowledge, and brings them up with its own young, looking after them with the same motherly devotion as its own brood, nurturing them in exactly the same way. The coot thus brings up the young of strangers, but we throw them out with the cruelty of an enemy.

¶The vulture is so called from its leisurely flight (a volatu tardo); because its body is so big it cannot fly quickly. Vultures, like eagles, can scent corpses from above the sea. They fly very high and can see much that is concealed by the darkness of the mountains. It is said that vultures have no carnal knowledge of the other sex, and that they conceive without male semen and without mating. Their offspring live to a great age, and often attain a hundred years; nor do they often come to an early grave. ¶What can those people say to this, who are accustomed to laughing at the mysteries of our faith when they hear that a virgin gave birth, and scorn such a birth as being impossible, because no man had harmed the modesty of an unmarried girl? They regard something as impossible for the Mother of God which, it cannot be denied, is to be found among vultures. A bird gives birth without a male partner, and no one can dispute it; but if Mary, as a betrothed virgin, gives birth, they question her virginity. But we warn them that the Lord, who is of her flesh, will affirm the truth. ¶Vultures are able to predict the death of man by certain signs. They learn from these signs, and when a lamentable battle is about to break out between two enemy armies, a great crowd of these birds follows the host and shows that many

men are about to fall in battle and become the
prey of vultures.

¶Cranes get their name from the creaking sound of their own voices. It is worth remembering how they set out on a journey. They submit to a kind of military discipline, and, lest the force of the wind should hinder them on the way to their chosen land, they swallow sand and weigh themselves down with gravel until they are heavy enough. Then they climb to a great height, so that by looking down from high up they can see the land which they are seeking. As they hurry on their way, they follow one leader, as Lucan says, 'until the letter is broken and disappears as the birds scatter' [Pharsalia v.716:

Palamides was said to have invented the alphabet by copying the figures formed by flocks of cranes in the sky]. ¶The leader knows the way, scolds lazy fliers, and keeps the line in order by his calls. If he becomes hoarse, another bird will take up his post. They are all of the same mind in looking after any birds who become weary, and gather round them to bear them up, until their strength is restored by resting. In the night the cranes keep careful watch. You can make out the watchmen in their places, with the rest of the flock sleeping; others go the rounds and look out for any enemies who might make a surprise attack. Their efforts ensure that all are safe. When the watchman has completed his allotted time he goes to sleep; but first he wakes one of the sleepers by calling to him, so that he can replace him. The new watchman takes over the task willingly, not like a man, who would do it in a bad temper and lazily because he wanted to go on sleeping. The crane comes quickly from its resting-place, and having enjoyed the benefit of his predecessor's watchfulness, carries out the task with equal care. The cranes divide the night into watches and arrange the sequence of watchmen according to strict rules, holding stones in their claws in order to ward off sleep. If there is cause for alarm, they call out.

¶The parrot is only found in India. It is green in colour with a pumice-grey neck and a large tongue which is broader than those of other birds, and which

enables it to speak distinct words, so that if you could not see it, you would think that a man was speaking. It will greet you naturally, saying 'Ave' or 'Chere' (the Latin and Greek words for 'Hail'). It learns other words if it is taught them. As the poet [Martial xiv.73] says: 'Like a parrot I will learn other words from you. I have taught myself to say "Hail, Caesar".' Its beak is so hard that if it falls from a height on to a stone, it presses on it with its beak and uses it as a kind of protection of extraordinary firmness. Its head is so strong that if you have to teach it with blows while it is learning how to speak to men, you have to strike it with an iron rod. For as long as it is young, not much over two years old, it learns what it is taught quickly and remembers it longer; if it is a little older it is forgetful and difficult to teach.

¶The charadrius (a kind of river-bird) is, so the naturalists say, entirely white, without the smallest black marking. The dung from its gut is a cure for weak eyes. You will find it in the courts of kings. If someone is sick, he will know from the charadrius whether he will live or die. If the man's illness is mortal, it will turn away its head as soon as it sees him, and everyone will know that he is going to die. If he is going to recover, the bird will look him in the face and take all his sickness on itself. It flies up to the sun, burns off the sickness, scatters it in the air, and cures the sick man. The charadrius is the figure of our Redeemer. For our Lord is wholly white, without a speck of black, 'who did no sin, neither was guile found in His mouth' [I Peter 2:22]. ¶When the Lord came to us from on high, He turned His face from the

Jews because of their unbelief and turned instead to the heathen, for 'surely He hath borne our griefs and carried our sorrows' [Isaiah 53:4]. He was raised upon the Cross, and 'when He ascended up on high, He led captivity captive, and gave gifts unto men' [Ephesians 4:8]. But you may object that because the charadrius is unclean according to the law, it cannot be likened to Christ. But John said of God: 'And as Moses lifted up the serpent in the wilderness, even so must the Son of Man be lifted up' [John 3:14]. And in the Law it says that 'the serpent was more subtle than any beast of the field' [Genesis 3:1]. The lion and eagle are unclean beasts, but they are likened to Christ because of their royal rank: the lion is king of beasts, the eagle king of birds.

¶Storks are called 'ciconie' in Latin because their cry is like that of the cicadas, and they make it with their beaks rather than their voice, using the clashing of their beaks. They are the messengers of spring, gregarious, enemies of snakes. They fly across the sea in great flocks towards Asia. These birds are said to have no tongues. Crows fly in front of them as leaders, and they follow like an army. Their love for their young is extraordinary. For they keep the nests so warm that their feathers fall out with the continuous incubation. The same length of time that they spend bringing up their young is spent in return by their offspring in caring for the parents. The stork signifies prudent men, careful servants of God; just as storks pursue snakes and draw off their poisons, so they pursue evil spirits who make poisonous suggestions, and reduce them to nothing. Jeremiah says: 'Yea, the stork in the heaven knoweth her appointed times; and the turtle and the crane and the swallow observe the time of their coming; but my people know not the judgement of the Lord' [8:7].

¶The heron (ardea in Latin) is so called because it flies to great heights (ardua); it hates rain and flies above the clouds to avoid storms. When it takes flight, it is a warning of a storm, and many people called it 'tantalus'. This bird is a symbol of the souls of the saints or of the elect, who, scorning the turbulence of this world, lest they should become ensnared in the traps of the devil, raise their minds above earthly things to the serenity of heaven where they see God face to face. The heron seeks its food in the water, but builds its nest in woods and trees. For even the just man takes his nourishment from fleeting things, but places his hope in rare and sublime matters. And though his life is sustained by this transitory world, his soul rejoices in the eternal. The heron will try to defend its chicks in the nest with its beak, to stop other birds from carrying them off. So the just man chastens with sharp words all those who try to deceive his subjects. Many herons are white, while others are ash-grey; both colours bode well, for white is the colour of innocence and grey of penitence. The innocent and the penitent belong to the same kin. The colour of the heron and its way of life are an example to all men of religion.

¶The Latin name of the swan is 'olor', the Greek 'cignus'. It is called olor because it has completely white feathers, and no one has seen a black swan;  'olon' is Greek for 'complete'. It is called cignus from its singing, because it produces sweet songs with a well-tuned voice. It is said that swans can sing so sweetly because they have a long curved neck, and to produce a good singing tone the voice must travel down a long curving path to give a variety of notes. It is said that in the far north, when the bards sing to stringed instruments, numbers of swans gather and sing together in harmony. Sailors regard them as a good sign; as Ovid's friend Aemilius Macer wrote: 'When you are telling omens by the appearance of birds, to see a swan always means joy; sailors love it because it never dives beneath the waves'. In moral terms, the white-plumaged swan represents successful deception; just as the white feathers hide black flesh, so dissimulation hides a sinful heart.

When the swan swims on a river it holds its neck
high, like a proud man drawn along by the vanity of
the world, who glories for a brief time in his posses-
sions. The story of the swans gathering around the
bards reminds us that those who live for their desires
seek out the company of like-minded men to satisfy
their lusts. But when at length the swan dies, it sings
very sweetly. ¶In the same way, when the proud
man has to leave this life, he still delights in the
sweetness of secular things, and remembers all the
evil he has done as he dies. When the swan is
plucked of its white feathers, its black flesh can be
seen, and it is roasted. In the same way, when the
proud rich man dies, he is stripped of worldly pomp
and goes down into the flames of hell, where he is
plagued with every torment: he who living used to
enjoy food is in turn made the food of the flames.

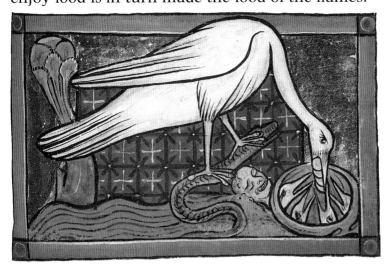

¶There is a bird called the ibis, which purges its stomach with its beak. It uses serpents' eggs and the corpses of animals to make a very welcome meal for its young. For it is afraid to go into the water, because it does not know how to swim, so it walks up and down the shore, day and night, looking for dead fish or other bodies thrown up by the water. It is the image of carnally-minded men, who make evil deeds their spiritual food, and nourish their pitiful souls with this food to their own destruction. But you, O Christian, reborn from water and the Holy Spirit, enter the spiritual waters of the mysteries of God, and eat of the most wholesome foods, of which the Apostle tells us, saying: 'The fruit of the spirit is love, joy, peace, long-suffering, gentleness, goodness, faith' and so on [Galatians 5:22]. If the sun and moon did not send out their rays, they would not shine. If the birds did not stretch out their wings, they could not fly. So you, O man, if you do not arm yourself with the sign of the cross and spread the wings of two-fold love, you cannot win through the storms of this world to the most safe haven of the heavenly home: 'And it came to pass, when Moses held up his hand, that Israel prevailed; and when he let down his hand, Amalek prevailed' [Exodus 17:11].

¶There is an animal called the assida, 'stratocame-leon' in Greek, whose real name is the ostrich. It has feathers, but it does not fly; its feet are like those of the camel. When the time comes for it to lay its eggs, it lifts its eyes to heaven and looks to see if the stars called the Pleiades have appeared; it will not lay its eggs until these stars have appeared. When, in about the month of June, it sees those stars, it digs in the earth, lays its eggs and covers them in sand. When it gets up from that place, it at once forgets them and never returns to its eggs. The peaceful weather seems to ensure that the heat of the summer will warm the sand and hatch the chicks. If the ostrich thus knows its proper time, and forgets its offspring, laying aside earthly things to follow the course of heaven, how much more, O man, should you turn to the prize of the summons from on high, for which God was made man, so that He will snatch you from the powers of darkness and set you with the princes of His people in the kingdom of His glory.

¶The coot is a clever and very intelligent bird, which does not eat dead bodies, does not fly about aimlessly, but lives in one place, remaining there all its life and finding its food and rest there. If all

believers behaved themselves and lived in this way, and did not wander off on strange paths as the heretics do, and did not seek secular desires and pleasure, but stayed in one place and rested in the Catholic Church, where the Lord makes them dwell together in harmony, they would have their daily sustenance, the bread of immortality, and the precious blood of Christ would be their drink. And he shall refresh himself with the most polished eloquence of the Lord, 'sweeter than honey and the honeycomb' [Psalm 19:10].

¶The jackdaw (graculus) is so called because of its garrulousness, not, as some say, because they fly in flocks (greges): it is obvious that it gets its name from its way of  speaking. It is the most talkative of birds, with a grating voice. It symbolises either the vain speeches of philosophers or the verbosity of heretics. What else can we say about them? Jackdaws signify gossips and greedy men. If you study greedy men, they gossip together after meals and tell tales. The jackdaw will flap through the woods from one tree to the next, cawing as it goes, like a talkative man who never ceases to repeat evil things about the neighbours among whom he lives. If a jackdaw sees someone go past, he will chatter, and if he finds something hidden he will do the same, because the gossip will not only slander men of the world, but also those hidden in places of religion. If a jackdaw is captured, it is shut up in a place where it can hear people talking, and it will learn to say words.

¶The halcyon is a sea-bird which brings up its young on the shore, and lays its eggs in the sand, around midwinter. It considers this to be the best time

to bring up its young, when the sea is at its highest, and its waves crash on to the coasts more wildly, because the bird's special quality can shine out all the better. For however fiercely the waves rage they will suddenly subside as soon as the eggs are laid, and the storm-winds will die down to a gentle breeze: the sea and the wind are calm when the halcyon hatches its eggs. They take seven days to hatch, after which the young come out, and the bird can leave the nest. It spends another seven days feeding them until they have grown. Do not marvel at such a brief period of feeding when the hatching takes so little time. This little bird has such magic that sailors can be certain that the calm weather will last a fortnight. These are called the 'halcyon days' and no trace of storm or tempest will darken them.

¶The phoenix is a bird from Arabia, so called either because its colour is like the dye from Phoenicia, or because it is unique in the

whole world. It lives for five hundred years, and when it feels itself growing old, it collects twigs from aromatic plants and builds itself a pyre, on which it sits and spreads its wings to the rays of the sun, setting itself on fire. When it has been consumed a new bird arises next day out of the ashes. It is a symbol of our Lord Jesus Christ, who says: 'I have power to lay down my life, and I have power to take it again' [John 10:18]. If the phoenix has the power to kill itself and bring itself to life, why, O foolish man, do you grow angry at the word of God who is the true Son of God. For our Saviour descended from heaven, and unfolded His wings, which were filled with the sweet scent of the Old and New Testament. He sacrificed Himself to God the Father on the altar of the cross, and rose again on the third day.

¶The phoenix is known to live in certain places in Arabia and to live for five hundred years. When it knows that the end of its life is approaching, it builds a chrysalis of frankincense and myrrh and other spices, and when it is about to expire it goes into the chrysalis and dies. From its flesh a worm emerges, which gradually grows up: in due course it grows wings and appears in the form of the previous bird. This bird teaches us by its example to believe in the Resurrection, for the Resurrection is an event without parallel, without the benefit of reason. The phoenix produces all the signs of the Resurrection; for the birds are there to teach man, not man to teach the birds. It is therefore an example to us that

the Author and Creator of birds does not suffer His
saints to die eternally, but wishes to restore them by using His own life-force. Who then has announced to this bird the day of its death, so that it makes its chrysalis and fills it with sweet scents and goes into it and dies, so that the scents can overcome the stench of death? O man, make your chrysalis, and putting off the old Adam, and all his deeds, clothe yourself in the new man. Your chrysalis and sheath is Christ, who will protect you and shelter you in the evil hour. Do you not wish to know why the chrysalis is a protection? He said: 'I have protected you with my quiver' [Isaiah 49:2]. Your chrysalis is therefore faith; fill it with the sweet soul of your virtues, that is, with charity, mercy and justice, and enter its depths, filled with the odour of your good deeds. The end of your life should find you clothed in this faith; so that your bones are as full of sap as a luxuriant garden, in which seeds are produced again and again. Know therefore the day of your death, just as Paul knew his when he said: 'I have fought a good fight, I have finished my course, I have kept the faith' [II Timothy 4:7]. And he entered into his chrysalis like a true phoenix, filling it with the odour of his martyrdom.

¶The 'cinnomolgus' is an Arabian bird, and gets its name because it builds its nest in the tall forests, in the cinnamon tree. Men cannot climb the tree because its branches break very easily, so they shoot

lead-weighted arrows into the twigs and pull the
cinnamon down. They sell it for very good prices,
because cinnamon is prized above all other wares.

¶Harz birds come
from the Harz
mountains in
Germany, which
give them their
name. Their
feathers shine in
the darkness, so
that, however

dark the night, they shine brightly if they are thrown
on the ground, and serve to light the way. With the
help of their shining feathers the way is plain.

¶When it sees its parents growing old and their eyes growing dim, the bird called the hoopoe pulls out their feathers, licks their eyes, and warms them until they are rejuvenated. It is as if it wanted to say: 'Just as you brought me up, so I want to do the same for you.' If beasts, without reason, do as much for each other, how much more should men, endowed with reason, care for their parents in return for their care in bringing them up, for the Law says: 'And he that curseth his father, or his mother, shall be surely put to death' [Exodus 21:17].

¶The pelican is an Egyptian bird which lives in the solitary places of the River Nile; and this is where it gets its name, because Canopus is the same as Egypt.

It shows exceeding love towards its young. If it has
brought offspring into the world, when these grow
up they strike their parents in the face. The parents
strike back and kill them. After three days, their
mother opens her own breast and side, and lies on
her young, pouring all her blood over the dead
bodies, and thus her love brings them back to life. So
our Lord Jesus Christ, who is the author and origin-
ator of all creatures, begot us, and, when we did not
exist, He made us. But we struck Him in the face; as
Isaiah said: 'I have begotten sons and raised them
up, but they have despised me'. Christ ascended the
Cross and was struck in the side: blood and water
came forth for our salvation, to give us eternal life.

¶The night-owl is so
called because it flies
around at night; it
cannot see by day.
As soon as it sees
the splendour of the
sunrise, it grows
weak. The night-owl

is the same as the screech-owl, but the screech-owl
is bigger. The night-raven is the same as the night-
owl, and loves the night. It is a bird which flees
from light and cannot bear the sight of the sun.

This bird signifies the Jews, who, when our Lord came to save them, rejected Him, saying: 'We have no king except Caesar', and preferred the darkness to the light. Then our Lord turned to the Gentiles, and shed light on those who sat in the shadows and in the shadow of death, of whom it is said: 'A people whom I have not known shall serve me.'

¶The screech-owl gets its name from the sound of its cry. It is a bird associated with death, burdened with feathers, but bound by a heavy laziness, hovering  around graves by day and night, and living in caves. Ovid says of it 'A sluggish screech-owl, a loathsome bird, which heralds impending disaster, a harbinger of woe for mortals.' [Metamorphoses v.550]: For among the augurs it was said to foreshadow evil. The screech-owl is an image of all those who yield to the darkness of sin and flee the light of justice. Hence it is counted among the unclean creatures in Leviticus. The screech-owl is the symbol of all sinners. ¶The screech-owl gets its name from its cry because its mouth speaks what overflows in its heart; what it thinks inwardly, it utters in its voice. It is known as a loathsome bird because its roost is filthy from its droppings, just as the sinner brings all who dwell with him into disrepute through the example of his dishonourable behaviour. It is burdened with feathers to signify an excess of flesh and levity of spirit, always bound by heavy laziness, the same laziness which binds sinners who are inert and idle when it comes to doing good. It lives by day and night in graveyards, just like sinners who delight in their sin, which is the stench of human flesh. It lives in caves; nor does the sinner cast off darkness but hates the light of truth. If other birds see it, they set up a great clamour, and it is vexed by their fierce onslaughts. So when a sinner is recognised in full daylight he becomes an object of mockery for the righteous. And if others catch him in flagrante delicto he will be severely reprimanded by them. They tear out his feathers and wound him with their beaks, because the righteous hate the carnal deeds of the sinner and curse his excesses. The screech-owl is called unhappy, because it is a truly unhappy creature through its habits which we have just described.

¶Sirens, so the naturalists tell us, are deadly creatures, which from the head down to the navel
are like men, but their lower parts down to their
feet are like birds. Their music is a song with the
sweetest melody, so that if seafaring men hear it
afar off, they leave their true course and are lured
towards the sirens. The sweetness of the sound
enchants their ears and senses and lulls them to
sleep. As soon as they are fast asleep, the sirens
attack them and devour their flesh, and so the lure of
their voices brings ignorant and imprudent men to
their death. In the same way all those who delight in
the pomp and vanity and delights of this world,

and lose the vigour of their minds by listening to comedies, tragedies and various musical melodies, will suddenly become the prey of their enemies.

¶The partridge gets its name from its call. It is a cunning and unclean bird. For the males mount each other and forget their sex in the grip of their lust. They are so treacherous  that one bird will steal another's eggs; but this betrayal is altogether fruitless. For as soon as the young hear their true mother's voice, their natural impulse is to leave their foster-mother and return to their true mother. ¶The devil imitates their example, trying to rob the eternal Creator of His offspring, and if he succeeds in gathering round a few fools who do not know what they are doing, he nourishes them with carnal delights. But as soon as they hear Christ's voice, they spread their spiritual wings and commend themselves to Christ.

¶Partridges equip
their nests with elab-
orate defences. They
clothe their dwelling
with thorn twigs,
so that any animal
which attacks them
is held back by the

sharpness of the brambles. The partridge covers its
eggs with dust, and returns to its nest by different
ways lest it should give away its whereabouts.
The females often carry off their young elsewhere
to deceive the males, who very frequently attack
the young if the females pay too much attention
to them. They fight at mating time, and the loser
must submit to sexual intercourse like a female. The
females are so lustful that the scent of the males
borne on the wind will make them pregnant. If a
man approaches their nest, the mothers will come
out and pretend to be wounded in their feet or
wings, so that they move slowly and appear to be
easy to catch. By this trick they manage to hold
off attackers and delude them into moving away
from the nest. The young are equally cautious:
when they are afraid of being discovered, they fall on
their backs and lift little pieces of earth in their

claws, and so defend themselves by concealing themselves so well that they lie hidden from detection.

¶Magpies or pies might be called poets, because they can speak words with different sounds, like men. They hang in the branches of trees,  calling with importunate chatterings, and even if they cannot form a language for speech, they can imitate the sound of the human voice. Someone once said, very much to the point: 'I, the chattering magpie, greet you as Lord with a steady voice; if you do not see me, you will deny that I am a bird' [Martial xiv.76]. The magpie is called 'Picus', after Saturn's son, because he used them in foretelling the future. It is said that this bird has something divine about it. The proof is that if a magpie is nesting in a tree, a nail or other fastening will not stay long in it, because it falls out as soon as the bird alights in the tree; but you can think what you like of this story. The sound of its voice may mean either the loquacity of heretics or the discussion of philosophers, as we said about the crow.

¶The sparrowhawk is stronger in spirit than in its talons, and has great strength in a small body. It is called 'accipiter' from 'capiendo', to seize. It is a bird that loves to seize other birds, and for this reason is called a hawk or raptor. Paul says: 'For ye suffer if a man bring you into bondage (accipit)' [II Corinthians 11:20]. They say that the sparrowhawk does not love its young. For as soon as it sees that they are trying to fly, it does not give them any food but beats its wings and drives them out of the nest, and so makes them seek their prey at a very young age, lest they become lazy when they are grown. It takes care that they are not idle when they are young, lest they abandon themselves to luxury, and become weak through ease, and expect food to be brought to them rather than hunting

for it. So it ignores the instinct to feed them in
order to compel them to dare to hunt their prey.
¶The hawk is the image of the holy man, who seizes
the Kingdom of God. It is written in the book of
Job: 'Doth the hawk fly by thy wisdom, and stretch
her wings towards the south?' [39:26]. However intelligent one of the elect may be, the Holy
Spirit will stretch out his wings by inspiring his
thoughts, and he will cast off his old raiment to take
flight by virtue of his new feathers. The hawk thus
may be considered to signify the renewal of the
Gentiles. ¶On the keeping of hawks: tame hawks
should be put in a safe warm place if they are
to moult properly. These places are called mews, and
wild hawks are put there and shut up in order to
make them tame. There they lose their old feathers
and put on new ones, just as a monk, once he is
confined to the cloister, will put off his previous
vices and adorn himself with the clothing of a
new man. Nor is the hawk allowed to go out until
the old feathers have been discarded and the new
ones have grown properly. When he is strong
enough to fly, he is released and will fly to hand.
In like fashion, if a new monk has to leave the
monastery he must turn his hand to good living,

and after that he will take flight until all the strength of his spirit is devoted to the desire for heavenly things. ¶Hawks are usually carried on the left hand, so that they fly to the right to seek their prey when they are let off the leash: 'His left hand is under my head, his right hand doth embrace me' [Song of Songs 2:6]. The left represents temporal things, the right everything that is eternal. On the left sit those who rule over temporal things; all those who in the depths of their hearts desire eternal things fly to the right. There the hawk will catch the dove; that is, he who turns towards the good will receive the grace of the Holy Spirit. ¶The hawk's perch signifies the rectitude of life under the monastic rule, because it is suspended high above earthly things, and separates monks from earthly desires. He who firmly holds to the statutes of monastic life sits bound to this perch. The perch is said to have two walls which support it at either end. These two walls are the active and the contemplative life, and they bear up those who lead an upright existence. ¶The hawk is accustomed to have jesses on its feet lest it takes the opportunity to fly away when it is released. Just as the feet of the hawk are humbled and restrained by jesses, so men are restrained by the fear of judgement and the pain of punishment. Joseph's feet were chained in shackles, just as the remembrance of present misery and eternal pain binds the soul lest it stray from righteousness. ¶The leash by which the hawk is tied to the perch is the mortification of the flesh, whichholds all new monks within the life of the monastic rule. It is called a 'corrigia' in Latin because it is made of the hide (corium) of a dead animal; and thus it signifies the mortification of the flesh. This leash is not broken, but is used when a hawk flies to catch its prey. In the same way, if a brother goes out to do business in the world outside, the leash of the rule is not broken, but when he returns binds him all the stronger.

¶The bat is an ignoble creature; it is called 'vespertilio' because it comes out in the evening (vesper). It is a flying creature, but is like four-footed beasts, and has teeth, which are not  found in other birds. It gives birth like four-footed beasts, and does not lay eggs but brings forth its young alive. It does not fly with the help of feathers, but uses the folds of its skin which bear it up and allow it to fly as if it had wings. These mean creatures have the habit of clinging to each other, and hanging like clusters of grapes. When the last one lets go, the whole group dissolves. It is a kind of mutual charity rarely found among men.

¶The nightingale gets its name because its song signals the end of night and the rising of the sun. It is a very alert watchman: if it is keeping its eggs warm with the heat  of its body, it comforts itself in its sleepless toil by singing sweetly. At least, this seems to me to be its intention, because it can hatch its young no less with sweet melodies than with the warmth of its body. The weak yet virtuous woman who carried a heavy stone lest her children should lack bread and nourishment, and tried to soften the harsh lot of poverty by her nightly songs, imitated the nightingale: even if she could not rival the sweetness of its song, she equalled its maternal devotion.

¶The raven gets its name from the sound of its voice, because it rasps. It is said of this bird that it does not feed its newly-hatched young properly until it can see that they  resemble itself and have the same dark feathers. As soon as it sees that their feathers are black, it recognises them as its own offspring and feeds them more copiously. It pecks the eyes out of corpses before attacking the rest of the body. ¶The raven signifies the blackness of sinners; as Solomon tells us: 'The eye that mocketh at his father ... the ravens of the valley shall pluck it out' [Proverbs 30:17]. The raven also signifies the Gentiles, as in Job: 'Who provideth for the raven his food? When his young ones cry unto God, they wander for lack of meat' [38:41]. Food is given to the young ones of the raven, the sons of the Gentiles, when they desire to be converted. The bird is also seen as a good symbol in the Song of Songs: 'His locks are bushy, and black as a raven' [5:11]. The raven is the blackness of sin or unfaithfulness; as the Psalmist says: 'He giveth to the beast his food, and to the young ravens which cry' [147:9].

¶The crow is a bird which lives to a great age. Its name is the same in Greek as in Latin: 'cornix'. They say that it can reveal the purpose of men's actions: it can disclose

the whereabouts of an ambush, and predict the future. This is a great offence, to believe that God entrusts His counsels to crows. Among other omens they are credited with foretelling rain with their cries. Hence the poet's words: 'The crow loudly cries for rain' [Virgil, Georgics i.388]. Men should teach themselves to love their children from the crow's example. When their young are learning to fly, they follow them assiduously, and in case they should weaken, they bring them food. They do not give up the task of feeding for a long while. By contrast, our women wean human children as soon as they can, even if they love them; and if the children are troublesome, they show a real aversion to breastfeeding them. If they are poor they throw out their babies and expose them, and if they are found, deny all knowledge of them. Even the rich would rather kill the child in the womb

for fear that their lands should be divided into
many parts, and use murderous juices to extinguish
the concealed pledges of their love; they are more
ready to take life away than to give it. Who apart
from mankind denies their offspring? What other
creature has such harsh treatment from its father?
Who made brothers unequal in their brotherhood?
The sons of the same rich man will have very
different fates: one will be entrusted with all his
estates, the other will inherit a poor and worked-
out corner of his father's lands. Did nature divide
the merits of the sons so unevenly? She divides
equally for all, giving them enough to be born
and to live. Nature should teach you not to make
any distinction in dividing an inheritance between
those who are equal by brotherhood of blood.

¶The dove is a simple
bird, free of gall,
which looks lovingly
at its mate. In the
same way, preachers
are free from rage
and bitterness,
because although
they may be angry, it
cannot be called rage

when they are angry with good reason. The dove sighs rather than sings; and so the preachers, not caring for love-songs, sigh for their own sins and those of others. The dove does not mangle things with its beak: again, this applies to the preachers, who do not falsify the Holy Scriptures as the heretics do. The dove chooses its grain, pecking out the best, just as preachers choose the best sentences from the Scriptures. It brings up the chicks of other birds: the preachers nourish the children of this world who are estranged from God by their sins, and bring them again to Christ. The bird sits near running water so that if it sees a hawk it can dive in and escape. In the same way the preachers have the Holy Scriptures close at hand, so that, seeing the devil attacking them with temptations, they can immerse themselves in the actions prescribed by Scripture and thus escape. The dove uses its wings to defend itself; and the preachers strengthen their defences with the words of the fathers. It nests in holes in the rock, just as preachers take refuge in their belief in the wounds of Christ, of which it is said: 'The rock moreover was Jesus'. They make a nest and a defence there for themselves and others. The dove can also recover from blindness: the preachers of the Holy Church, if some gift of the Holy Spirit has been lost through a person's sin, recover it just as David recovered the gift of prophecy which he had lost. It flies in flocks, just as the preachers who believe in the faith gather in flocks and follow good works. For such good works as we do are steps towards God.

¶The turtle-dove gets its name from its call; it is a shy bird, which lives on mountain-tops and lonely places in the desert. It avoids the houses and com-pany of men, and lives in the woods; when the leaves fall in winter, it lives in hollow tree trunks. It covers its nest with the leaves of squills to protect it from attacks by wolves, because it knows that wolves avoid this kind of leaf. It is said that the turtle-dove, as soon as it loses its partner and is widowed, hates the idea of marriage and the marriage-bed. For her first experience of love has betrayed and deceived her in the death of the loved one, who is now eternally unfaithful; and this is bitter to the memory because the grief caused by death was greater than the delights of love. So she refuses any new match, and will not dissolve the oaths and bonds that tie her to her dead mate. She continues to love him alone, and to keep the name of wife for him only. ¶Learn, O women, how precious widowhood is, if birds set such store by it. Who set down these laws for the turtle-dove? If I search for man's hand in this, I cannot find it. No man would dare to do it, not even St Paul; he did not set out rules for widows, but said only: 'I will therefore that the younger women marry, bear children, guide the house, give none occasion to the adversary to speak reproachfully' [I Timothy 5:14]. And elsewhere he says: 'But if they cannot contain, let them marry: for it is better to marry than to burn' [I Corinthians 7:9]. Paul wishes women to do as the turtle-dove. And elsewhere he urges young people to marry, because our women are not capable of living as chastely as the turtle-dove. God gave the turtle-dove this grace and lasting love, and provided her with the virtue of restraint. The turtle-dove does not think of revoking its first vows of fidelity, because it knows how to preserve the chastity which it pledged at its first mating.

¶The swallow gets its name because it does not feed while on the ground, but catches and eats its food in the air. It is

a talkative bird, and flies in swift turns and circuits.
It is very careful and far-sighted in building its nest
and bringing up its young, because it avoids great
heights from which its young might fall. It is not
troubled by birds of prey, and is never killed by them.
It flies across the sea, and spends the winter there.
The swallow is a very small bird, but shows exceptional devotion; it makes good use of everything,
and its nests are more precious than gold, because
they are wisely built. 'How much better is it to
get wisdom than gold!' [Proverbs 16:16]. What is
cleverer than to possess the unbounded freedom of
flight and to entrust one's home and offspring to the
houses of men, where nothing will attack them? For
it is good to see how the young are accustomed to
the company of men from the day they are born, and
hence are safe from the attacks of creatures that prey
on birds. The swallow skilfully builds its carefully-
designed dwelling without any assistance, gathering straw with its beak and daubing it with mud to
hold it together. Because it cannot carry the mud
with its feet, it dips the tips of its wings in water,
which it sprinkles on to the dust and so turns it to
mud; with this it glues together the straws and twigs
which it has gathered. It builds the fabric of its whole
nest in this way so that its young can move around

in it as safely as if they were on solid ground; they cannot catch their feet in the woven texture and do not suffer from cold when they are still young and tender. Such careful workmanship is indeed common to most birds; but the swallow is exceptional in the loving care and outstanding cleverness of its intelligence and observation. It also has some skill in healing, because if the young are threatened by blindness or their eyes are hurt, it possesses a means of healing by which their vision can be restored.

¶Quails are so called from their cry; the Greeks call them 'ortigias' because they were first seen on the island of Ortygia. They travel at set times. When summer is over, they cross the sea, in a flock led by the 'ortigometra'. When a sparrowhawk sees this bird approaching land, it tries to seize it, and for this reason the others do their best to protect it and to keep it safe from all dangers. Their favourite food is poisonous seeds, which is why the ancients forbade the eating of this bird. This is the only creature,

apart from man, to suffer from the falling sickness.
The quails also have their set time of arrival, because as soon as summer is over they fly across the sea. ¶The heat of summer is the warmth of love, the winter frost the time of spiritual numbness. From his love of Christ and his neighbours, the just man crosses the sea of this world to the love of God, so that he can always remain in its warmth. He who burns with love within wishes to avoid the frost of winter, that is, the storms and winds of unexpected temptation. The leader of the flock is called 'ortigometra', whom the hawk seizes when he sees it approaching land. The earth is earthly pleasure, the seas the dangers of this world. The hawk is the devil, lurking in order to tempt us. Just as the hawk seizes the quail as it approaches land, so the devil uses those who approach earthly things out of greed as lackeys, because those who seek earthly things either for themselves or to fulfil the needs of their brethren will be seized by the hawk, that is the devil; they despise spiritual things in favour of earthly delights. So everyone should choose a good leader, who will avoid such dangers from the outset. There are two kinds of men, good and evil. Evil men are best at outward things. So just men choose evil men as their leaders, and observe their actions closely. By

paying attention they can detect the first leanings towards sin, and avoid them accordingly. This bird suffers, like men, from the falling sickness, because sin befalls the holy man just as much as the man of the world. He does not die whenever he sins, because the grace of repentance is not denied to him. So it is written: 'For a just man falleth seven times and riseth up again' [Proverbs 24:16]. For as often as a just man sins, he strives to rise again.

¶The goose bears witness to its watchfulness at night by its noise. No other creature can scent man so keenly as the goose. Because of their cries, the Gauls who assaulted the Capitol were captured: as Rabanus says, they stand for provident men, watchmen who take their task in earnest. There are two kinds of geese, wild and tame. Wild geese fly high and in strict order, and symbolise those who live remote from earthly rank and follow an ordered life. The tame geese live in villages, and call the whole time; they often wound each other with their beaks. They symbolise those who are happy to lead a communal life, but give themselves up to gossip and slanderous talk. Wild geese are always grey in colour, and I have never seen a multi-coloured or white one. Tame geese are not only grey, but also multicoloured or white. The wild geese are always ash-grey because you will find the grey cloak of repentance among those who live far from the world. Just as a goose will be aware of a man's scent before other animals, so clever men will distinguish others from a distance by their good or evil reputation. If a goose scents a man approaching it will continually call in the night, for if a brother finds negligence and ignorance in others, it is his duty to cry out. The cry of geese on the Capitol was once very useful to the Romans; and in our chapter the daily cry of the watchful brother, when he detects negligence, frightens off our old enemy the devil. The cry of geese saved Rome from enemy attack, the outcry of the watchful brother protects the common life from disturbance by evil-minded men. Divine providence would not have revealed the natural qualities of birds so clearly if we had not been required to gain some advantage from it.

¶The peacock gets its name from the sound of its voice; its flesh is so hard that it scarcely putrefies, and it is very difficult to cook; someone once said of it: 'You

marvel, whenever it opens its jewelled wings, how anyone could be so hard-hearted as to give this bird to a cook' [Martial xiii.70]. Solomon brought a peacock from distant lands, with varied colours in its feathers; it signifies the Gentiles, coming from the ends of the earth to Christ, who adorns them with the grace and splendour of many virtues.

¶The screech-owl (ulula), 'apo toi olozin' in Greek, is so called from its mourning and lamentation. When it cries it imitates either weeping or groaning. So augurs held that when it lamented it foretold disaster; if it was silent, it heralded prosperity.

This bird signifies the wailing of sinners in hell, and, as the prophet says when he speaks of the destruction of Babylon: 'Their houses shall be full of doleful creatures, and owls shall dwell there, and satyrs shall dance there' [Isaiah 13:21].

¶The Greeks call the bird hoopoe because it lives among human dung and feeds on filth and excrement. It is an altogether revolting bird,  with a distinctive crest; it is always digging around in graves and human dung. If you smear yourself with its blood before you go to sleep, you will see demons that will threaten to suffocate you. ¶Rabanus says that this bird signifies evildoers, men who love to dwell in the filth of sin. The hoopoe is said to love sorrow, because the sorrow of the world brings about the death of the spirit; and for this reason all who love God must always rejoice and pray without ceasing, give thanks in all things, because joy is the fount of the spirit. The naturalists tell us that when the hoopoe grows old and cannot fly, its offspring comes to it and plucks out the old feathers from its parent's body. It does not cease to care for its parent and feeds it until the new feathers grow, as the Scriptures say; once its strength is restored, it can fly again. It is an example to perverse men, who, when their parents grow old, throw them out of their own houses and refuse to maintain those, old and now feeble, who nourished them when they themselves were young and weak. A thoughtful man should learn from this thoughtless creature, which (as we have described) supports its parents in old age, the duty that he owes to his father and mother.

¶The cock gets its name because it is sometimes castrated. This is the only bird whose testicles are cut off; the ancients used to call eunuchs cockerels. They say that  its limbs, if they are mixed with liquid gold, will be eaten away by it. The crowing of the cock is a pleasant sound at night, and not only pleasant but useful, because, like a good neighbour, it wakes the sleeper, encourages the downhearted, and comforts the traveller, by charting the progress of the night with its melodious voice. When it crows, the robber leaves his ambush, the morning star itself awakes and lights the sky. The anxious sailor no longer fears for his life, and the storms which the winds of evening often arouse die down again. The devout go to their prayers at cock-crow, and can read their books once more. When the cock crew thrice, the rock of the Church was cleansed of the guilt he had incurred by his denial of Christ before cock-crow. Its song brings hope back to everyone, eases the pain of the sick, cools the fevered brow, brings faith back to those who have lapsed. Jesus watches over those who stray, and brings the wanderers back to the path; He looked at Peter and his sin at once vanished and his denial was forgotten in the penitent recognition. For we are taught that nothing happens by chance, but everything is done by the will of the Lord. [This passage is based on the hymn 'Aeterna rerum conditur' from the Breviary.]

¶Hens are symbols of divine wisdom, as Christ Himself said in the Gospels: 'O Jerusalem, Jerusalem, thou that killest the prophets, and stonest them which are sent unto thee, how often would I have gathered thy children together, even as a hen gathereth her chickens under her wings' [Matthew 23:37]. The name of hen is not an insult: compare it with other birds. Many birds hatch and rear chicks, but no other bird is so enfeebled by its chicks as the hen. If we see swallows, geese or storks off their nest, we would not know that they had chicks, but if we see a hen off the nest we can tell by the weakness of her voice and her ruffled feathers that her changed appearance means that she is broody. Because the chicks are weak, she makes herself weak. Because we grew weak, so the wisdom of God made itself weak and became flesh and dwelt among us.

¶The duck, 'anas' in Latin, gets its name from its love of swimming (natandi). Some kinds of duck are called German, and these fatten better than the rest. The goose  gets its name from the duck ('anser', from 'anas') either because they are similar or because both love swimming. Geese mark the hours of the night by the sound of their voices. It was through their cackling that the Gauls' attack on the Capitol was discovered. ¶All species of birds are born twice. For first the egg is born, and then the chick is formed by the warmth of the mother's body, and given life. They are called eggs because they are full of moisture. Things that have moisture on the outside are simply damp, but if they have moisture within, they carry life in them. Many think that the word ovum, egg, comes from the Greek; the Greeks say 'oa' for eggs, leaving out the middle letter. Many eggs are conceived by empty wind; nothing is hatched from them, unless they are conceived in a mating with a male bird and pene- trated by the spirit of his seed. The properties of eggs are such that wood that is soaked in eggs will not burn, and clothing will not catch fire. Mixed with chalk, they will glue pieces of glass together.

¶Sparrows (passeres) are very small (parvi) birds: hence their name. They are both small and weak. As it is written in the psalm: 'Yea, the sparrow hath found an house' [84:3]; elsewhere: 'As a sparrow alone upon the house-top' [102:7]; and in another place: 'Flee as a sparrow to the mountain' [11:1]. Sparrows represent holy men in another psalm: 'Where the sparrows make their nests' [104:17]. The sparrow is very quick and swift, and cannot abide in the woods, but eagerly seeks its home in the cracks in the walls: when it finds such a place it rejoices greatly, because it will no longer need to beware of the snares of its enemies. Thus the soul rejoices when it sees that a dwelling has been prepared for it in the kingdom of heaven. Likewise the sparrows which are prescribed in Leviticus as offerings to cleanse leprosy represent the sacrament of Christ's passion. For in this 'the living sparrow and the cedarwood, and the scarlet and the hyssop' are dipped [Leviticus 14:6]. But the living sparrow, which we must understand as the divinity of the only-begotten Son, is also dipped in water and the blood of the slaughtered sparrow, that is in the grace of baptism. For we are not baptised into the passion of one man, but into the passion of God and man.

¶The kite is weak both in strength and flight: its Latin name (milvus) comes from 'mollis avis' (weak bird). It is nonetheless very rapacious and always attacks tame birds. The kite signifies, I think, the rapacious or proud man, as in the passage in the psalm: 'The kite's home shall be in the fir-tree.'

¶Bees (apes) are so called because they hold on with their feet, or because they are born without feet (pedibus). Later they grow both feet and wings. They are eager workers at their task of making honey, each with a specific task and dwelling assigned to him. They live in homes built with indescribable skill, and make honey using different blossoms. They fill the castles made with wax with their innumerable offspring. They have an army and kings; they fight battles; they flee from smoke, and are angered by noise. They are known, by observation, to be born from the corpses of oxen. In order to obtain bees, the flesh of dead calves is beaten; from its putrefying blood worms emerge, which later become bees. So the insects that come from cattle are called bees; those that come from horses are hornets; mules produce drones and donkeys bring forth wasps. The larger worms in the outer cells of the honeycomb are called 'castros' by the Greeks; others think that they should be called kings, because they command the castles (castra). Only the bees, among all creatures, have a shared offspring, a shared dwelling, a shared home under the same sky, shared toil, shared tasks, shared produce of their labour, shared flight. What else? Their origin is shared, as is the purity of their virgin bodies, and their birth is shared, since they do not take part in sexual intercourse, nor are they torn by the pangs of birth; yet they have a host of children. They choose a king, create their own people, and although subject to a king are nonetheless free. For they maintain his right to judgement and are devotedly faithful to him because they recognise him as their elected leader, and honour his great responsibility. The king is not chosen by lot, for a lottery is ruled by chance rather than judgement. And often the mad chance of fate

will prefer the worst to the best. With bees, the king
is naturally endowed with special qualities, as his large and handsome body shows, and – the most important virtue in a king – his friendly nature. He has a sting, but does not use it in revenge; for there are laws of nature, not written down in letters, but innate in custom, that those who have unlimited power should be all the milder in their punishment. But those bees who fail to obey the royal laws inflict their own punishment on themselves, and die by their own sting, just as even today the people of Persia hold that they must expiate their crimes by carrying out their own death sentence. So no race on earth serves their king with such reverence and devotion as the bees, not even the Persians, who have the harshest laws for their king's subjects, nor the Indians, nor the Sarmatians. No bee dares to leave its hive and set out in search of food unless the king has gone first and is leading the flight. The flight of the bees takes them over scented country-side, where flowers grow in the gardens, little streams murmur through the meadows, and plea-sant banks beckon. There children play their lively games, there men take exercise on broad meadows, there all cares fall away. The foundations of the bees' fortress are made from their toil among flowers.

¶The perindens is a tree found in India; the fruit of this tree is very sweet and pleasant, and doves delight in its fruit and live in the tree, feeding on it. The dragon, which is the enemy of doves, fears the tree, because of the shade in which the doves rest,

and it can approach neither the tree nor its shadow.
If the shadow of the tree falls to the west, the dragon flies to the east, and if the shadow is in the east, the dragon flies to the west. If it finds a dove outside the shadow of the tree, it kills it. ¶The tree is God the Father, the shadow God the Son; in Gabriel's words to Mary: 'The Holy Ghost shall come upon thee, and the power of the Highest shall overshadow thee' [Luke 1:35]; the wisdom of the Lord is a heavenly fruit, that is, the dove or Holy Ghost. Watch therefore, O man, that you do not escape from eternal life after you have received the Holy Ghost, the spiritual dove of reason; and that, as a stranger to Father, Son and Holy Ghost, the dragon who is the devil does not kill you. Beware, O man, and dwell in the Catholic faith, and hold fast to the Catholic Church. Keep watch, as far as you are able, that you are not caught outside its doors and seized by that old serpent the devil and devoured, just as Judas, as soon as he left the Lord and his brother apostles, was at once devoured by a demon and perished. ¶The serpent is the name for all snakes which can fold themselves back and roll up. It is called 'anguis' because it goes in a curving (angulosus) track and never straight. It is also called 'coluber' because it inhabits shadows (colit umbras) and

because it draws itself along with much slippery winding. For anything which slips away when you try to hold it is called slippery, like a fish or a snake. It is called a serpent because it moves in a hidden way, without obvious paces, but with minute movements of its scales. Creatures like the lizard and salamander, which have four feet, are not snakes, but reptiles. Snakes are reptiles which go on their belly and breast. There are as many poisonous snakes as there are different kinds of snake and as many deadly snakes as there are colours among them.

¶The dragon is larger than all the rest of the serpents
and than all other animals in the world. The Greeks
call it 'dracontam', and from this comes its Latin
name 'draco'. It is said that it is often tempted to
come out of caves into the air, and the air is shaken
by it. It has a crest, a small mouth and narrow
nostrils, through which it breathes, and it puts out
its tongue. Its strength is not in its teeth, but its tail,
and it harms more by blows than by force of impact.
It has no harmful poison. But it is said that it does
not need poison in order to kill, because it slays
anything which it embraces. Not even the elephant,
with its huge body, is safe from it. It lies concealed
near the paths which elephants are in the habit of
using, entangles their feet with its coils and suffo-
cates them to death. Its homes are Ethiopia and
India, where there is always heat. ¶This dragon is
like the devil, the fairest of all serpents, who often
leaves his cave to rush into the air; the air glows
because of him, because the devil rises from his
abyss and transforms himself into an angel of light,
deceiving fools with hopes of vainglory and human
pleasures. The dragon has a crest because the devil
is the king of pride; its strength lies not in its teeth
but in its tail, because having lost his power, the
devil can only deceive with lies. It lurks on the paths

which elephants use because the devil lays the coils of sin in the path of all those who make their way towards heaven and kills them when they are suffocated by sin. For if anyone dies in chains of guilt, he will without doubt be condemned to hell.

¶The basilisk's name in Greek (regulus) means little king, because he is the king of creeping things. Those who see him flee, because his scent will

kill them. And he will kill a man simply by looking at him. No bird that sees him can fly past unharmed: it will be consumed at a distance by his fiery breath and then swallowed. But he can be conquered by the weasel, and for that reason men put weasels in the holes where basilisks live. If the basilisk sees the weasel, he flees, but the weasel pursues him and kills him. For the Creator of all things has made nothing for which there is not an antidote. The basilisk is half-a-foot long, with white spots. He lives in dry places, like the scorpion; if he comes to water he poisons it so that those who drink get hydrophobia and are struck with panic. The hissing snake is the same as the regulus, killing by his hissing before he bites or scorches. ¶But the basilisk signifies the devil, who openly kills the heedless sinner with his venom; he himself is conquered, like all other harmful creatures, by the soldier of Christ who puts all his hope in the Lord, whose power overcomes and tramples underfoot all hostile forces. Of this too the prophet says in the Psalms: 'Thou shalt tread upon the asp and basilisk; the young lion and the dragon shalt thou trample underfoot' [91:13]. This represents divine power, which holds sway over so many savage creatures. All these names are aptly bestowed on the devil. He is an asp when he strikes secretly; a basilisk when he spreads his poison abroad; a lion when he pursues the innocent; a dragon when in his evil greed he swallows the heedless. But, truly, at the glorious coming of our Lord, all creatures will lie subject at His feet. He alone was strong enough to subdue these fierce creatures, who is coeternal and consubstantial with the Father in His divinity. If we trace these things in the preaching of the holy fathers, so that we are not led astray by any depraved heretics or madmen, every one of these sayings is true.

¶The viper is so called because it gives birth under duress (vi pariat). For when its belly feels the pangs of birth, its offspring do not await their  natural release in good time but bite through the mother's body and break out, killing the mother. It is said that the male puts his head in the female's mouth in order to release his semen; she, in her sexual ecstasy, bites the male's head off; and so both parents die: the male in mating, the female in giving birth. St Ambrose says that the viper is the most evil of all creatures and more cunning than all other serpents. If it is overcome by sexual desire it goes to the seashore and seeks an eel; it hisses to attract the eel and to invite it into its conjugal embrace. The eel does not refuse, and grants the poisonous snake the mating which it seeks. ¶The embrace of the viper and the eel counterfeits nature; it is not done according to the laws of true species, but in the heat of passion. O man, learn from this; anyone who tries to

seduce another man's wife may well embrace a
snake. He hastens to the snake which has found its
way into his bosom not by the path of honesty and
truth, but by the slippery slope of a devious love. He
hastens to her who takes back her poison like a
snake, for snakes are said to suck back the poison
they spit out once their coupling is complete.

¶The asp (aspis) is so called because poison flows
in when it bites and spreads (spargit) through the
body. The Greeks call the poison 'ios' and the asp
gets its name because it kills with a venomous bite. It
moves with its mouth open and steaming. There are
various kinds and families of asps, which inflict
differing degrees of harm. It is said that if an asp

notices a snake-charmer trying to entice it with melodies intended for that purpose and lure it out of its hole, and it does not want to come out, it will lay one ear on the ground and stop up the other with its tail so that it cannot hear the magic sounds and is not forced to go where the snake-charmer wants. ¶The asp is like the men of this world, who stop up one ear with the desires of this world. The other they stop up with the sins they have committed, in order not to hear the voice of the Lord. Asps, at least, only stop up their ears; these men close their eyes, so that they will not see heaven and be reminded of the work of the Lord. The dipsa is a kind of asp called in Latin 'situla', because whoever it bites dies of thirst (sitis). The ypnalis is a kind of asp that kills by sending its victim to sleep. Cleopatra applied this kind of asp to herself, and at once slipped into sleep and death. The emorrosis is an asp that makes its victim sweat blood. If you are bitten by it, your veins open and your life drains away with your blood. The prester is an asp which goes around with its jaws wide open and steam coming from its mouth. If this creature attacks, the victim's whole body swells up and he dies; the body putrefies at once. The horned snake (cerastes) gets its name because it has horns on its head like rams' horns. It has a kind of fourfold

growth which it displays in order to attract animals
which think that it is good to eat, and then it kills
them. For it conceals its whole body in the sand, and
gives no sign of life. If birds or other creatures take
up the bait, it catches them. It is much more flexible
than other snakes, and appears to have no spine.

¶The snake called
scitalis has such a
brightly-coloured
back that all
creatures that
approach it slow
down to admire
its splendour. And
because it is too

lazy to pursue its prey, the snake captures it by its
extraordinary appearance. It is so hot that even in

winter it will
expose its glowing
body in the open
air. Lucan says of
it: 'Only the scitalis
will now lay out its
body in the harsh
chill of the frost'
[Pharsalia ix.717].

¶The amphisbaena is so called because it has two heads, one in the right place, the other on its tail. It goes in the direction of both heads, and its body forms a circle. [This passage clearly baffled the artist as well!] It alone of all snakes moves around in the frost and is the first to come out of hibernation.

¶In the waters of the River Nile there lives a creature called the idrus; 'hydros' is the Greek word for water, and the idrus is a water-snake. Those who are bitten by it swell up; this is often called 'ox-sickness' because it can be healed by cattle-dung. The water-snake is a many-headed dragon, like the one on the island, or rather marsh, at Lerna in the province of Arcadia. But we know that the hydra was a place where water gushed out, destroying the neighbouring cities; when one spout was closed, many others broke out. Hercules, seeing this, drained the swamp, and so he stopped the flow of water. For the hydra is so called from water. The hydrus is a fierce enemy of the crocodile; when it sees a crocodile sleeping on the shore with its mouth open, it goes and rolls in the mud so that it can glide all the more easily into its jaws. The crocodile at once swallows the snake alive. The latter eats the intestines of the crocodile and thus gets out alive and completely unharmed. ¶So death and hell are like the crocodiles, and their enemy is the Lord Jesus Christ. For, taking on human flesh, He descended into hell and destroyed its intestines, and led out all those whom it unjustly detained. He dealt a deadly blow to death itself when He arose from the dead, and the prophet mocked death, saying: 'O death, I will be thy plagues; O grave, I will be thy destruction' [Hosea, 13:14].

¶The boas is a snake found in Italy. It is very heavy and follows the flocks of sheep and cattle, and hangs from their udders. It sucks them dry and kills them; because it slays oxen (boves) it is called boas.

¶The iaculus is a flying serpent, mentioned by Lucan [Pharsalia ix.720]. They perch in trees  and when their prey approaches, they throw themselves down on it and kill it; so they are called iaculi, or 'throwing-snakes'.

¶In Arabia there are white serpents with wings, called sirens, which run faster than horses, and are also said to fly. Their poison is such that the victim is dead before he feels the pain of their bite.

¶The seps is a small snake, whose poison does not consume just the body, but the bones too. The poet depicted it thus: 'the wasting seps, dissolving bones and body together' [Pharsalia ix.723].

¶The dipsa is said to be such a small snake that you do not even see it when you tread on it; its poison kills before you feel it. Those who die this instant death have no trace of sadness on their faces. The poet says: 'Aulus ... was bitten by the dipsa on which he trod, its head thrown back, and he felt hardly any pain, nor did he feel the bite of its teeth' [Pharsalia ix.737].

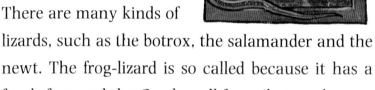

¶The lizard is called a kind of reptile, but it has limbs. There are many kinds of lizards, such as the botrox, the salamander and the newt. The frog-lizard is so called because it has a frog's face and the Greeks call frogs 'botraca'.

¶The salamander is so called because it is proof against fire; it is the most poisonous of all poisonous creatures. Others kill one at a time; this creature kills several at once. For if it crawls into a tree, all the apples are infected with its poison, and those who eat them die. In the same way, if it falls in a well, the water will poison those who drink it. It is the enemy of fire and alone among animals can put out flames. It lives in the midst of flames without pain and without being consumed; not only does it not burn, but it puts out the flames.

¶The saura is a lizard which, when it grows  old, goes blind. It creeps into a crack in the wall and looks towards the east, into the rising sun, and by this means regains its sight.

¶The newt (stellio) gets its name from its colouring, because its back is covered in shining spots like stars (stellae). Ovid says of it: 'It bears a name … derived from the multi-coloured spots which star its body' [Metamorphoses v.461]. It is such an enemy of scorpions that the very sight of it strikes terror into

them and they are transfixed. ¶There are other
kinds of serpents such as admoditae, elephantia,
camedracontes. There are as many names for them
as they have different kinds of deadly poison. All
serpents are by nature cold, and can only harm
when they become warm. For as long as they are
cold, they will not touch anyone. So their poison is
more harmful by day than by night. In the frost of
the night they lose their strength, because they
become cold in the dew at night. They gather the
vapour in their bodies, for they are pests which are
cold and freezing by nature. Hence in winter they
sleep in nests, and go out in summer. So if anyone is
overcome by a snake's poison, he is at first stupefied
and then, as the poison warms up and begins to take
effect, it at once kills him. Venom is so called because
it runs in the veins. When the poison is injected into
the veins, it is increased by the natural action of the
body, and disturbs the spirit. Hence venom can only
harm when it is mixed with the blood. Lucan says:
'The poison of the serpent destroys when it mixes
with blood' [Pharsalia ix.614]. All venom is cold,
and so the soul, which is fiery, flees the coldness of
the venom: the sharpness of the serpent's senses
stands out. We read in Genesis: 'Now the serpent
was more subtle than any beast of the field' [3:1].

¶The snake has three habits; the first of these is that when it grows old its eyes grow dim and if it wants to renew them, it starves itself and fasts for many days until its skin grows

loose. Then it looks for a narrow crevice in the rocks. It wriggles into it and sloughs its old skin. And we through many tribulations put off the old Adam for Christ's sake and seek Christ the spiritual rock, and find a narrow fissure, that is, the strait gate. ¶Its second habit is that when it comes to a river to drink water, it does not take its poison with it, but leaves it behind in a pit. When we come together to hear the heavenly word of God in church, we must leave behind our earthly body, that is, earthly and evil desires. ¶Its third habit is that if it sees a naked man, it is frightened, but if it sees him clothed, it attacks him. In spiritual terms, the serpent was unable to attack the first man, Adam, for as long as he was naked in paradise, but when he was clothed, that is, his body became mortal, then it attacked him.

¶The scorpion is a land worm; it belongs with worms rather than serpents; it is armed with a sting; and it gets its name from Greek, because it

stings with its tail and spreads its poison in a gaping wound. The scorpion has this property, that it stings the palm of the hand. ¶The scorpion signifies the devil or those who serve him. Hence the saying in the Gospel: 'Behold, I give unto you power to tread on serpents and scorpions and over all the power of the enemy' [Luke 10:19]. And the Lord also said: 'If a son shall ask bread of any of you that is a father, will he give him a stone? or if he ask a fish, will he for a fish give him a serpent? or if he shall ask an egg, will he offer him a scorpion?' [Luke 11:11–12]. There are three things needful to us, faith, hope and charity: faith, so that we truly believe; hope, so that we always await with due patience those things that God has promised us; charity, so that we love Him eagerly and zealously, with all our hearts and minds and all our strength, and our neighbours as ourselves. The fish is the sign of faith, the egg that of hope, and the bread that of charity; on the other side, the stone is harshness, the serpent faithlessness and the scorpion despair. In the water of baptism we receive faith; hope is like an egg, for we cannot see the chick inside it and yet we expect it to hatch; and charity, because it is all-powerful, is like bread.

¶The horned ser-
pent is a snake
which gets its
name from the
horns on its head,
which are like
those of rams. It
is called 'cerastes'
in Latin from the
Greek word 'cer-

asta' meaning horns. For it has four little horns, and by pretending that they are something which can be eaten, it kills animals. For it buries its whole body in the sand, and gives no clue as to its whereabouts except for those horns, with which it lures and captures birds and animals. It is more flexible than other snakes, and does not appear to have a spine. The cerastes lies in the road and bites the heels of horses, so that they rear up, and their riders fall off.

¶The worm is an animal which is born of flesh or
wood or any material thing without mating: but
nonetheless worms are born from eggs. But they are
either of the earth, of water, of air, of flesh, of leaves,
of wood or of clothing. Spiders are worms of the air,
so called because they live on air, which produce
from their slender bodies long threads, and, always
busy with weaving, they never cease from their
labours, perpetually occupied with their craft. The
land centipede is so called because of its many feet;
they roll up into a ball and live in jars. The leech is a
water-worm which gets its name ('sanguissuga',
bloodsucker) because it sucks blood, and lies in wait
for those who are thirsty. When it attaches itself to
the mouth or any other part of the body, it sucks
blood, and when it cannot hold any more, it spits out
what it has swallowed in order to suck fresh blood.
¶The silkworm is a leaf-worm, out of whose weaving silk is made; it is so called because it empties itself
while it makes the thread, and only air remains
inside it. The caterpillar is a leaf-worm found on
cabbages or vines; it is called 'eruca' because it
erodes the leaves. It rolls itself up and does not fly
around like a locust, rushing hither and thither and
leaving things half-eaten, but remains until the fruit
has been destroyed and as it crawls slowly on its way

it eats everything in small mouthfuls. The Greeks call a kind of woodworm 'teredo' because they eat as they bore (tereo). We call them termites, but in Latin they are called woodworms, and they hatch from fallen trees at unfavourable times. The worm found in clothes is called a moth; it tunnels into them until it can find somewhere to eat holes. Then there are the worms that come from flesh. 'Enigramus' is a worm in the head; 'lumbicus', the stomach-worm, is a tapeworm, so called because it is found in the lumbar region. Lice are worms of the flesh, and get their name (pediculi) because they have feet (pedes). Fleas or 'pulices' get their name because they come from dust (ex pulvere). The tarnius is found in pork. Ricinus is a worm that attacks dogs, and fastens itself to their ears; 'kynos' is the Greek for a dog. The usia is found in pigs; it irritates them (urit) and this gives it its name. The place where it bites is so irritated that blisters form. The bug is so called because it is like a plant which has the same unpleasant smell; but it is really a worm that is born of rotten flesh. A worm does not move with ordinary steps or by using its scales like a snake, because it has no spine, unlike the snake. Instead it moves by stretching its body out and then pulling it together, repeating this movement as it goes.

¶Fishes (pisces) get their name, like cattle (pecus), from the word for grazing (pascere). They are reptiles which swim, and are called reptiles because they have the same appearance and nature. Although they can dive into the depths, they still move in a creeping motion as they swim; for this reason David says: 'So is this great and wide sea, wherein are things creeping innumerable' [Psalm 104:25]. Some kinds of fish are amphibians, which can walk on the land and swim in the sea. 'Amphi' in Greek means both: they live on both sea and land, like seals, crocodiles, and hippopotamuses. ¶Cattle and the beasts of the field and of the air were given names by men before fishes, because they saw them first. As men learnt little by little about the kinds of fishes they were given names, often from their similarity to creatures on land, such as frogs, calves, lions, blackbirds and peacocks with many-coloured backs and necks, and thrushes with white and other colours. Other fishes were so called because their ways were like those of creatures on land: dogfish were called after dogs, because they bite; wolves got their name because they pursue other fish voraciously. Others were named after their colour: shad, because they are the colour of shadows, dories because they are golden (French, 'doré'), varies, from their variety of colour, which common folk call trout. Some got their name from their shape, like the orb, a round fish which is nothing but a head, and the sole which is like the sole of a shoe.

¶There is a monster in the sea which the Greeks call 'aspidochelon'; the Latin 'aspido' is a tortoise; it is also called sea-monster because its body is so huge. It was this creature that took up Jonah; its stomach was so great that it could be mistaken for hell, as Jonah himself said: 'Out of the belly of hell cried I, and Thou heardest my voice' [Jonah 2:2]. This creature raises its back above the waves, and it seems to stay in the same place. The winds blow sea-sand on it and it becomes a level place on which vegetation grows. Sailors believe it is an island, and beach their ships on it. Then they light fires, and when the creature feels the heat of the fire, it dives into the water and drags the ship down with it into the depths. The same will befall those who are full of unbelief and know nothing of the wiles of the devil, trusting in him and doing his work; they will be plunged into the fires of Gehenna with him. The nature of the monster is such that when it is hungry it opens its mouth, and gives out a sweet scent; the little fishes smell this and gather in its mouth. When the monster's mouth is full of fishes it closes its jaws and swallows them. The same will befall those who are not firm in their faith, and yield to all delights and temptations as if drunk with scents; and then the devil swallows them up. ¶Whales are creatures

of a huge size, which draw in and spout out water.
They make greater waves than any other sea-creature. The male of the species is called musculus; the females conceive by mating with him.

¶There is a monster in the sea called the serra, or flying-fish, which has huge wings. When the serra sees a ship in full sail on the sea, it raises its wings and tries to keep up with the ship for four or five miles; but it cannot keep up the pace and folds its wings. The waves carry the wary creature back into their depths. The serra is like the things of this world, while the ship is the image of the just man, who sails unharmed and without shipwreck through the storms and tempests of this world. The serra which could not keep up with the ship signifies those men who at the beginning set their hand to good works, but cannot continue in them, and are overwhelmed by all kinds of vices, which drag them into the depths like the waves of the sea. 'He that endureth to the end shall be saved' [Matthew 10:22].

¶The dolphins are so called because they follow men's voices, or gather in shoals when music is played. There is nothing swifter in the sea. They often leap over ships in their flight; if they go in front of the ship, leaping in the waves, they appear to foretell bad weather. They are also called 'simones'.